working sex

Sex Workers Write About a Changing Industry

edited by
annie oakley

SEAL PRESS

Working Sex
Sex Workers Write About a Changing Industry

Copyright © 2007 Annie Oakley

Published by
Seal Press
A Member of Perseus Books Group
1700 Fourth Street
Berkeley, CA 94710

9 8 7 6 5 4 3 2

Library of Congress Cataloging-in-Publication Data

Working sex : sex workers write about a changing industry / edited by Annie Oakley.
p. cm.
ISBN-13: 978-1-58005-225-2
ISBN-10: 1-58005-225-8
1. Prostitutes—Biography. 2. Prostitutes—Social conditions.
3. Prostitution—History—21st century. I. Oakley, Ann.

HQ118.W67 2008
306.7409'045—dc22
2007039519

Cover and interior design by Domini Dragoone
Printed in the United States of America
Distributed by Publishers Group West

This book is for the ones who blazed the trail.

contents

Introduction 7
Annie Oakley

The Fisherman 14
Amber Dawn

Porn Piece 23
Bruce LaBruce

Smile, You've Just
Been Dominatrixed 30
Ana J

Trick 41
Chris Kraus

Yeoman Johnson 52
Juba Kalamka

The Ballad of Burt Starr 57
Michelle Tea

Devices: A Short Play 79
Naima Lowe

Staged... 86
Janelle Galazia

Sugar & Me 91
Mirha-Soleil Ross

Pimp 97
Tre Vasquez

Bella... 102
Shoshana Von Blanckensee

College Graduate
Makes Good as Courtesan................. 124
Veronica Monet

Campus Sluts Forever! 131
Jessica Melusine

An Interview with Gloria Lockett......... 138
Siobhan Brooks

Boys Stink.. 160
Blake Nemec

Meeting Rita 163
Eileen Myles

The Night that Plays Like
Ping-Pong in My Head 175
Mattilda, a.k.a. Matt Bernstein Sycamore

Degrade 178
Emi Koyama

Jimmy... **180**
Nomy Lamm

Golden.. **193**
Ariel Smith

Advice **196**
Kirk Read

My First Porn Film **202**
Jennifer Blowdryer

Dear John **211**
Mirha-Soleil Ross

Hello.. **219**
Sister Grimm

Anacam **225**
Ana Voog

My Stripper Year................................... **242**
Stephen Elliott

Songs.. **250**
Vaginal Davis

House Call **257**
Aiden Shaw

My Pride and Broken Buzzers............ **264**
Anna Joy Springer

Whoreanomics **277**
Shelby Aesthetic

introduction

Annie Oakley

One time in the olden days when I was working at the peep show (gateway drug to prostitution) a man came in who'd made the rounds of most of the girls but never seen me. I walked into my side of the scrubby booth known as the Victorian Parlor (complete with ye olde lounge-style lawn chair) and started the lame boob-rubbing moves that were always the prequel to the removal of my shirt. The guy wasn't interested and motioned for me to knock it off and come closer to the glass. He had some greasy piece of paper that he was fiddling with. It looked like it was about a thousand years old and had been used to wrap a hamburger. He unfolded it and pressed it to the glass for me to squint at.

"Do you know what this is?" he asked, looking at me intently and already rubbing his crotch through his jeans. It was some kind of clipping from a magazine, folded so many times that only mere molecules of the photo were left in between the web of white creases. I couldn't even muster a guess.

"It's the Partridge Family school bus! I want you to pretend like you're driving the Partridge Family school bus!" Not naked, not speaking lewdly about Danny Partridge, just with my feet on the glass and my hand on the invisible gearshift, making motor sounds. It was an easy $20 for five minutes of my time, and eventually he got passed off onto Carrie, a nightshift girl who really did drive a school bus during the day. Jackpot.

That's the story I used to trot out when people would ask me what was the weirdest customer experience I'd ever had. Which was always the first question they'd ask upon finding out what I did for a living (if they didn't immediately change the subject), followed closely by "How much do you make?" The Partridge Family guy wasn't even really the weirdest, but the real answer would've been a lot less interesting, and clearly people were digging for the entertaining. It made the job sound funny and light, like I spent the whole day indulging harmless adult children (hey . . . wait . . .). The kooky specificity of a Partridge Family bus fetish let them off the hook somehow, reassured them that their own weird desires were at least not that weird, and freed them from having to imagine themselves in the customer's role. Titillation without incrimination. This is the kind of story that Americans most want to hear from people who work in the sex trade, and consequently this is the kind of story that most often gets told, when anything gets told at all.

There are a few different ways one's story is allowed to be entertaining: funny, sexy, tragic, scandalous. Repentance, marriage, college graduation, lurid death, or a piece of investigative journalism are the favored endings. The rigid boundaries of archetype, be they happy hooker or downtrodden whore, are a kind of invisibility. They are one-dimensional. Should the story twist to the side you'll see nothing at all. Once marked by telling the story, you are branded for life. Your credibility is gone, you are forever seen in the context of the work. You don't get to go back to being a civilian. Who needs that kind of shit? People remain silent. This silence, this invisibility, is the linchpin upon which rests the glorious suspension of disbelief that is at the core of nearly every transaction in a service economy. It's the intellectual sleight of hand where one denies oneself knowledge of the essential personhood of the provider of a service or the maker of a product so as not to impede one's enjoyment of the product or service. In this way one avoids being implicated in the boredom, poverty, or ugliness of the work of the service provider. In late capitalist America under the rule of market logic, suspension of disbelief becomes almost a survival skill.

The sex industry is a huge industry. Think of all the venues: Internet porn, magazines, phone sex, dirty movies, strip clubs, peep shows, and hookers from the street, upscale agency, or the ad in the back of your edgy local weekly. Estimates put the U.S. sex industry at around $12 billion annually and growing rapidly, and the number of people presently employed in it at upwards of six million. To say nothing of those who have been a part of it in the past. What are the implications of the invisibility of such a huge segment of the population? What does it say about us as sexual consumers that we prefer our product to be anonymous? In a probably accidental rare moment of lucidity, former Surgeon General C. Everett Koop observed to ABC News that the sex industry "is making billions of dollars a year, is spreading to cable television and to the Internet, and yet their employees are considered to be throwaway people." When you refuse to recognize someone's humanity, you don't have to worry about their working conditions, their safety, their health, their ability to make a decent living. Thus the cops, pimps, club owners, and minimoguls at the head of petty fiefdoms like the Girls Gone

Wild porn empire get to run the industry with little outside interference or regulation. Not only is this bad for the people who work in the industry, but are pimps, police, and Joe Francis who you really want to trust with the shaping of the national libido?

Sex workers telling stories, humanizing ourselves through the sharing of experience and insight, punctures the bloated dream of consumption without consequence. It puts a real face on the mythological creatures that are the subject of so much fantasizing and demonizing. It moves us from a weird landscape populated by the iconography of people's fears and desires to a tangible, relatable reality; and only from there can we begin to be taken seriously as people deserving of safety, agency, and respect.

a t one point when I was taking a break from the sex industry, I became a housecleaner. My friend and I worked together, cleaning up after grown adults and fomenting cheerful resentment. It wasn't long before we knew who among our clients had an alcohol problem, who refused to have sex with her husband, who wore a padded-butt man-girdle, who was trying his hand at the newspaper personal ads. Nobody ever told us these personal details, nobody ever really told us much besides when to show up and what to use on the floors. A lot of stuff becomes obvious quickly when

11

you're observing people to whom you're invisible—and when you occasionally go through their drawers. The point is, the help always knows more about the boss than the boss knows about them. Sex workers are in a unique position to observe. The work takes place in a freakish crucible of the dynamics of race, class, gender, and sexuality. The fact that, by and large, we are relegated to a simple mascot position in public dialogue about these dynamics is a critical mistake.

Occasionally an academic will be thrown our way to spend a year slumming for a story, or someone will publish a memoir, but more frequently self-representation is a luxury we are denied. How would we represent ourselves if given the opportunity? In ten years of working in the business and meeting other whores, the one thing that's become apparent is that none of us can agree on a take on any aspect of the work. Even within ourselves, feelings and convictions can shift several times over the course of a night. Sometimes you see the best of people and yourself, and everything seems so easy and attainable, and the money feels like it's rolling in for free. Other times it's the worst job you've ever had and you can't believe the ugliness of humanity and you want to get out and never come back. The sex industry encompasses so many variations on how to get to the punchline of ass showing (domination! hooking! lap dances! let me count the ways!) and so many kinds of people who get into it for such different reasons and with different options for getting out. The possible experiences in the sex industry are so complicated and contradictory, there is no way to describe it without a multiplicity of voices. *Working Sex* includes pieces that clash not just in content but also in form. Experienced or experimental, poetic or pornographic, angry or academic, the pieces complement each other, and through their differences begin to articulate a fuller picture of the amazing humans who populate the mysterious landscape of this business.

the fisherman
Amber Dawn

You can sit in a whorehouse and breathe, until the stink of cigarette smoke and fried delivery food, of rubbing alcohol and latex and cheap scented candles, of hairspray and afro sheen, of cock and cunt everywhere disappears, and you think you are breathing fresh air.

You can talk with the girl wearing only a bra and panties while she dumps Cover-Girl foundation over her stretch marks (from childbearing), two scars (botched boob job), and knife wound (compliments of her man) about matters of the heart and decide that she is definitely, yes definitely, giving you sound advice.

You can help that same girl lift a drunken man off of the bed and carry his sloppy body out the door into the parking lot. You can watch her rifle through his pockets for money before leaning him up against the hood of his own car.

You can wear her clothes when she feels like being nice to you. Dresses that are nothing more than a tiny tube of shiny fabric. Dresses so small that either your ass is half-exposed or your nipples are popping out.

You can levitate six inches from the floor, held up by clear plastic stiletto heels and the ability to ignore aching feet.

You can do all of these things and not really feel like a whore. You can even jerk off a few men who close their eyes and say nothing to you. Afterwards you can rub the money in between your index finger and thumb not yet realizing that, indeed, you are a whore.

Such is the state of Sharon Margaret Murphy, thirty-seven years of age, purple glitter lipstick, asking herself, "Shouldn't this feel more dirty?" But Sharon is only six days new to Eve's Escape Massage and Steam. And during those six days Sharon mostly paraded around in borrowed outfits, watching the other younger girls break and turn. Really though, more important than any of this, Sharon has Chloe to paint her toenails and flat iron the bad perm from her hair, Chloe to share soda and *Cosmo* quizzes and stories about men and demons from the past. Sharon has Chloe to make prostitution feel like one big slumber party.

Now there is one characteristic inherent to a slumber party—that after some time the dawn will come. Today, Sharon's sixth day in the profession, the dawn came in the form of Chloe stumbling back into the staff room, wrapped in only a towel, her lipstick moved from her mouth to a smudge across her chin. Her blond bombshell clip-on ponytail a limp mess, like roadkill, in her left hand. Sharon's eyes grow wide with concern. Chloe flashes a quick smile; she is not looking for sympathy.

"Lookin' pretty tight, Chlo. Like you been fucked raw or somethin'," says Tia Lee without turning away from the *The Jerry Springer Show*.

"I can't do it," Chloe says, "I've been in there two hours already. And he wants to extend again."

"Who?" asks Sharon.

"The Fisherman." Tia Lee lazily points the remote at the TV, turning up the volume.

"He's got money still," Chloe says.

"I ain't going in there," Tia Lee states flatly. I already saw him once today. I had to pretend I couldn't speak English just to get out of that room. Tell him to go back to the fuckin' sea. Or send her." She waves the remote in Sharon's direction.

"What's wrong with him?" asks Sharon.

"He's got coke dick," says Tia Lee flatly. "And he talks, you know what I'm saying, 'tight pussy wet pussy pink pussy chocolate pussy my fingers in your pussy pussy fuckin pussy' the whole time. Caress says he pissed on her this one time. One minute she is pulling it, right, then the next he is just fuckin pissing everywhere. Sick shit if you ask me."

"Come meet him!" Chloe grabs Sharon's wrist and starts to pull her from the sofa.

the Fisherman sits on a wicker chair that is too small to hold a man his size. Naked but for a white hand towel thrown over his groin. Curls of black hair cling to his chest like algae to rock. The salt smell of sweat floods the room.

"I have to go home now. I brought the new girl to see you," says Chloe. "You be nice to her, okay, treat her like a lady." Chloe picks up a billfold from the nightstand. "So you'll be staying another hour then?" she asks. The Fisherman starts to tug himself under the towel. Scratching his nose with his other hand, he takes a series of quick short breaths. His eyes seem to be going in two different directions, one on Sharon and the other on his billfold. "I'll just get the money out for you," Chloe pulls out two brown bills, slow and deliberate for the Fisherman to see she's not pinching an extra hundred.

"Only half an hour," he says in a gurgly voice as his

towel drops to the floor. He shakes his near-erection in his hand. "I'll tire this old girl in no time."

"Okay," says Chloe. "I'll just give her two hundred to start off with. That's fair." She holds up the money, then places the billfold back on the night table. She smiles weakly as she gives the money to Sharon, and the room darkens as she closes the door. Sharon notices all the table lamps have been moved to the floor. The lighting throws the Fisherman's shadow up the wall onto the ceiling.

"Come here," he says. Sharon takes a step forward.

"Take off your dress." Sharon pulls herself out of the tight Lycra dress.

"You don't wear a bra?" the Fisherman asks, eyeballing her puckered nipples.

"Most of the time I do," Sharon starts to explain.

"You're not wearing one now because you want me to think you're a dirty slut." He nods deliberately as says this.

After years of being made to watch bad pornography with ex-boyfriends, Sharon is aware that there is only one possible reply,

"That's right. I am a dirty slut."

The Fisherman flops his dick in her direction and she comes to him. She grabs a condom from her purse, and with some effort, stuffs his limp dick into it. Sharon has never blown bagged limp dick before. She tries to compare it to something. A mouthful of water balloon? No. A bag of melted Smarties? Hmm . . . No. Maybe a sock monkey's arm. She decides that she prefers hard over soft. Soft is too hard to control. It goes wherever it wants, butting up against her back molars, picking a fight with her tongue. The Fisherman pushes on Sharon's head.

"All the way in," he groans. "Get it nice and hard for me. You want the big cock. Tell me how much you want it."

"I want it," Sharon mumbles, holding the Fisherman's dick in between her teeth as she speaks. Her forehead, now a receptacle for his sweat, slaps against his stomach. Her knees become one with the cheap shag carpet. She watches the clock from her peripheral vision, the second hand barely moving. And just when her gag reflex makes her eyes start to water the Fisherman's dick solidifies. Suddenly, he is standing upright. Knocks Sharon onto the floor.

"Get on the bed," he says, stepping over her. Sharon, dizzy from the ebb and flow of sucking cock, scans the dark room for a bottle of lubricant. The Fisherman slaps the mattress with one hand, his other hand clutching his balls.

Aware that the condom's lubricant has been completely sucked off, and equally aware that she is so repulsed by this bloated man, perspiring brine and beached upon the bed, that her vagina has sealed itself shut, Sharon searches the room once more, then gives in to his urgency. She lies down and spreads her legs.

"Pussy," says the Fisherman as he rolls on top of her. Then, as Tia Lee forewarned, the pussy mantra begins: He describes different colors and shades, states of pussy being, pussy synonyms, and three word subject-verb-object sentences, the subject always being pussy, such as pussy squirting juice, pussy eating cock. Except that Sharon's pussy wasn't eating anything. Sharon's pussy spat out the Fisherman's waning erection minutes ago. She reaches down and tries, unsuccessfully, to redirect him. Holding it in her hand she waits for it to come to life once more. It doesn't. Still, the Fisherman marches on to the beat of the pussy. Sharon does not ponder the strength of imagination that allows the Fisherman to feel that he is giving it to her hard and nasty. She does not decide that he is a liar, or a fool, or practicing some sort of bastardized tantric meditation. Instead she opts to join him. To abandon this ship of failed erections and half-hour time slots and dive into the deep blue of her mind.

It is an uneasy transition from reality to fiction. Although Sharon finds herself briefly in daisy fields and flying through space, she keeps returning to her soggy and dismal position beneath the Fisherman. She looks up at his face, sees a ring of dried blood around his left nostril, and shivers. She closes her eyes and tries to sing to herself. Sadly, the theme song from Flipper gets stuck in her head. Then, from somewhere, a slow and heavy tempo descends upon her. A rock anthem from the not-too-distant past beckons her like a pied piper of disassociation. There is no resistance, she gives herself to the dark rhythmic guitar and precision drumming . . .

Everything seems different. Now the shadow of him moving repetitiously on top of her is a dance of dark and light, of purples and greens upon the ceiling. Her legs, spread so wide, now span the entire room, knocking down walls, kicking holes in the roof, letting the stars fall in to the room. And there is Chloe, flashing beautifully behind Sharon's eyes. And when there is Chloe, Sharon feels her pelvic muscles tighten and her back arch. The Fisherman, still held in her left hand, has managed to flop his way inside her inner lips. Her clit aches from the friction. Sharon wonders, *Maybe this is what it's like to fuck another woman.* The sweet and painful wanting between her legs. The weight pressed against her body. Images of Chloe come faster than Sharon can manage. She touches the Fisherman's skin, and it is soft, and it is hers. A mix between a moan and a gasp of shock leaves Sharon's lips. She tries to recover, desperately inserting images of Jon Bon Jovi and Rambo's glistening brow. But Chloe is unmoving. Chloe with the tiny baby hands and squeak-toy laugh. Chloe whose lips move as she reads her books of poetry in the staff room. Chloe who squeezes Sharon's arm when she is excited. Chloe going round in her head like a chant. Like the Fisherman's pussy mantra. *Pussy . . . Chloe . . . pussy . . . Chloe . . . pussy . . .* Without the money and the clock ticking and words like whore and trick, they are just two people held captive by unrealized desire, doing whatever they can to break free. *Pussy . . . Chloe . . . pussy . . .*

porn piece

Bruce LaBruce

Sauntering into an international magazine store recently, I caught a glimpse of a row of a dozen magazines with covers graced by scantily clad females posing in provocative positions which would tend to signify, by the conventions of almost any civilization on earth, pornography. I took a few steps back and looked up at the store's sign to check that I hadn't wandered into a dirty bookstore by mistake. But no, it was indeed a regular retail outlet selling mainstream periodicals. When exactly, I though to myself luridly, did the world become so smutty? I felt my cheeks flush. Could I, Bruce LaBruce, international pornographer, be blushing?

Well, actually, let's not forget that I am, according to the title of my premature memoirs published a few years back, The Reluctant Pornographer, which may explain my ambivalence toward the notion of pornography taking over the free world.

Let's get one thing straight, or at least as straight as an intercontinental homosexual icon can manage: I don't watch porn. I don't collect it, I don't keep tabs on the latest porn stars and their exploits, I don't even incorporate it into my sex life. One reason for this may be that like many gay men I tend to live my life as if I were a porn star anyway, so passively watching it becomes almost redundant. Another reason may be that I encounter enough "found pornography" in the regular world, those quotidian ad hoc images which can be utilized as jack-off material: black gangbangers, clothes scissored off, operations in the emergency room of Trauma: Life in the ER, for example, or Eddie, the hot, one-legged house member of Big Brother lying shirtless in bed, or, in a pinch, even good old-fashioned men's gymnastics. I find these images, or the amateur pornographic self-portraits that everyday people send me over the Internet, much more sexually stimulating than your average adult entertainment video.

But wait a minute—I'm a porn star. Or at least, as someone who has made a number of sexually explicit avant-garde films in which he has performed oral sex and sodomy, I've been stuck with the epithets "porn star" and "pornographer." Shouldn't I be steeped in a world of split beaver, gang bangs, and leather slings? And shouldn't I be immune to the moral ambiguities engendered by such staples as bestiality, rape fantasies, and snuff?

It's a strange phenomenon that since I crossed that dark threshold into the adult netherworld, that ethereal region inhabited only by those who have dared to commit their sexual practices to celluloid or videotape for public consumption, I'm not supposed to blush or get embarrassed or presumably feel any other normal human emotions, especially vis-à-vis sex. For me, nothing could be further from the truth. Although I consider myself merely an artist who works in pornography, it's still a world that I've had to negotiate through, and I've discovered it's not one in which you can survive for long without a normal set of human responses, and yes, a strong moral compass. With so much emphasis lately on the mainstreaming of pornography and on the blurring of the line between art and porn, very little attention is being paid, particularly by those who are indulging in it, to the depth and darkness of the sexual imagination and the implications of toying with the dark side. The multibillion -dollar porn industry, which nonetheless still operates as a kind of dirty little secret, is nothing less than an adjunct of the collective unconscious, and to bring it to the surface, to mainstream it, may be unleashing something we're not prepared to handle. Think Pandora's box.

Back in the last decade, when gender studies and postmodern courses on desire introduced academics to the milieux of sex trade workers and pornographers, there was a tendency to overvalue these phenomena and to confer iconic status on their denizens. Some academics I knew in fact literally segued into various sex trades as part of their research, often with disastrous results. The making of pornography or the practice of prostitution unavoidably becomes a demystifying experience whereby one learns quickly that there is nothing particularly noble or glamorous about getting fucked for money. As I stood on the set of my first "legitimate" porn movie and found myself obliged to walk over and wipe the ass of one of the performers who was experiencing a little anal leakage, I didn't feel particularly glamorous. Once a participant in the sex trade, you must also be prepared for the inevitable wall of moral disapprobation that you will at some point run up against, a cold disapproval that may come from the most surprisingly liberal sources. Factor in all the other annoying occupational hazards—STDs, emotional instability, the ubiquity of drugs in the industry—and you may find yourself longing, like Kim Novak in *Bell, Book and Candle*, for a life a little more humdrum.

But I reckon today we're supposed to be beyond all these

mundane, practical considerations. The debate raging now is about aesthetics, about how pornographic images are mediated in the mainstream, and about the lexicon that has developed to accommodate this imagery. It's all very trendy.

I'm quite willing to bracket everything I've said thus far about pornography (I certainly didn't intend to be an alarmist) and consider the aesthetic dimension for a moment, because I think that's what ultimately civilizes porn and makes sense of it. The fact that 95 percent of the pornography that is produced today is unwatchable pap can be directly attributed to the advent of video and the concomitant decline of aesthetics. When pornography was being produced exclusively on film in the '60s and '70s, the emphasis on camera style and narrative and the formal mediation of content—the artistic considerations—were easily as important as the capturing of the sexual moment, which today has become the singular, all-consuming focus.

The digital revolution in general has ushered in an era of literalism, an unimaginative unity of style and substance that reduces meaning to a set of monolithic stylistic imperatives devoid of any complex interplay between the two. The notion that formal aspects may engage content in such a way as to produce contradiction or paradox or synthesis has been subsumed by the slavish capitulation of meaning to technology and production, to pure form. This is probably one of the reasons why the signifiers of the mainstream entertainment industry and of the adult film industry have started to become somewhat indistinguishable. Their shared fixation on the means of production instead of on the production of meaning has resulted in a somewhat dumbed-down, sexually extreme aesthetic proven to be the most commercially viable: sex sells. Mainstream stars and porn stars alike are forced to conform to the same hypersexualized image, regardless of the nature of the product they're currently promoting. It's a bland standardization of sexuality which has little or nothing to do with liberal or progressive attitudes towards sex.

So for me, when talking about the new incorporation of pornography into art and the mainstream, considerations of desire and pleasure, whether sexual or aesthetic, have become a little outdated and naive. ("Desire," like "gender," seems like such an antiquated, '80s term today—just a phase, I suppose, like the hula hoop.) My initial motivations for getting into pornographic representation, back when I was a punk in the '80s making underground fanzines and experimental Super-8 mm movies, were not only aesthetic, but also political and, well, revolutionary. I was a sexual idealist. My work since has been as much about the intersection of race and class with homosexual representation as about the filming and photographing of hot, sexy boys, as much about examining sexual stereotypes and iconography as about getting off. I can't deny that there was pleasure in the text, but the text itself was always easily as important. Audiences today, however, are so inured to the blandification of extreme sexual imagery that it no longer has that same kind of subversive impact. It's just meat now.

smile, you've just been dominatrixed

Ana J

My phone pounded and flashed from the coffee table. "Welcome to the Jungle" was blaring, which meant Ellen was calling. I decided not to answer. I'd been sitting on my couch for the past ten minutes, staring at the ripped seam of the throw pillow on my lap. I felt ugly and cartoonish. I tried to laugh to myself out loud, but it sounded contrived. I rolled my eyes. I lifted up my arms and put them down again. I wasn't sure what I was supposed to be doing.

It had been one hour since Darren came by to drop off my black and pink shoes. The broken ones with the permanent scuff marks around the heel. One hour ago, he threw his real genuine silver ID bracelet into the street. It slid across the pavement and disappeared into the darkness. The ID bracelet had been a gift from his grandmother, who had been recently murdered. He immediately regretted the hastiness of his decision. We had been repeating ourselves. Our argument, as usual, seemed unauthentic.

I was sitting in the middle of the alley, in an olive and beige canvas foldout chair. The chair was his, and I was giving it back. It was recently retrieved from my basement, where it had been buried underneath a pile of burnt-out tiki torches. It was now time for us to give each other's things back. He was slumped against the ledge of a very low window. Due to the complaints from my downstairs neighbor, we had transplanted our theatrical argument to this alley half a block down the street.

I was yelling, saying that he never really knew me at all. He looked distracted and said something totally unrelated. He reached into his pocket. His hand was clenched tight around something shiny. He held it out to me anxiously. I stood up and threw my cigarette on the sidewalk. He wasn't listening to me. He never really did. He only liked hearing the sound of my voice when I was angry. Or watching my eyes when I spoke.

"I don't want that. Whatever it is, I don't want it," I said angrily. I turned and began to walk toward my house.

"Please, take it." he begged.

I pictured him standing behind me with his arm out-stretched, and I wanted to run. I knew he had thrown it even before I heard the tiny metal chain rattle across the concrete. I listened to it slide across the ground for a moment, then stop. He sighed dramatically, and then there was silence. I quickly walked up the steps to my building and locked the door behind me. I was still for a moment, listening for footsteps, but there were none. I slumped with relief.

darren had been studying up on professional domi-nation every night for the past four weeks. He had finally come to the conclusion that our disaster of a for-mer relationship had been nothing but a scam. He decid-ed that he had been tricked, that I had tricked him. That I had "dominatrixed" him without his consent. It was hard to take it seriously at first. I had no idea that he had been spending hours on his computer every night. I didn't know that he had been scheduling fake appointments with local mistresses, making elaborate inquiries, trying to figure out exactly what a guy could expect for $250 an hour.

Then the text messages started. He bombarded me dai-ly with ridiculous messages, each one more offensive than the last:

"Yeah, power fucking destroy men, makes us love you so you can ruin our lives. Really fucking cool, yeah feminism."

"I only want to be with you, I'm sorry I can't make you happy."

"Sorry my dick was not big enough to make you a powerful strong woman. If I kill myself you will be truly fucking powerful. I loved you, and I am shit to you."

I never meant to tell Darren I was a dominatrix, I just blurted it out one day. It was late afternoon, and we had spent most of the morning at the beach. We were buying beer at the corner store, on our way to a barbeque. While we were in the store, I smiled at him and said, "You know, I feel like we are really starting to be friends, and it's nice."

He smiled and looked distracted. "Did you know I used to be a dominatrix?" I said to the back of his head as he reached into the cooler and grabbed a six-pack. He closed the glass door slowly. I felt my stomach tighten. For some reason I wanted to laugh, but didn't. Instead, I quickly told him I that I was retired. That I had just done it for a while a few years ago. And that I didn't really do it anymore. And that was that.

I was, of course, still working professionally at the time. Very much so. I had been throughout most of our relationship. It was, I firmly believed, my right to take care of myself. That was my business, and it was none of his. As a matter of fact, I had no interest in discussing my job with anyone.

As far as I was concerned, there was nothing to discuss. Especially not with him. The thirty-two-year-old emotionally unstable alcoholic. The adult infant. Just telling him that I was a retired dominatrix had been such a fiasco. He didn't have the capacity to understand. So I made a choice. You see, I did actually like him. In fact, I helped him. I confronted him constantly, even though I knew he would repeat his behavior. Like a client, confrontation made him feel better. He asked me to please help him get his life under control. To show him how to behave. He actually said that. He said I was the only reason he had stopped drinking, even though I knew that he hadn't. I played along even though I smelled beer on him all the time. I pretended not to notice. I accepted his generic displays of affection. That's what made him happy. He gave me rides. He bought me things. He felt needed. I thought we had a mutual understanding. I never lied about my feelings for him. He just didn't believe me. He wanted something different.

"Welcome to the Jungle" began to blare from my phone again. This time I answered. "Where you been, bitch?" Ellen demanded. "Ugh, these shoes are driving me crazy today. What are you doing on Sunday? Jim is in town, and he wants to see both of us."

Jim is in his late forties, and he enjoys business casual. Jim has been embezzling money from the company for years.

Ellen and I find this out one day by eavesdropping on a private phone call. We don't know what to do with this information. On the one hand, we could do the right thing and turn him in. We might be rewarded with a hefty bonus or a promotion. But on the other hand, this is the kind of information that people would kill to protect. Some people would do anything to make sure their secrets are kept. And I mean anything.

Ellen and I think about this. We discuss it over coffee. We have a girly pajama-party-and-pillow-fight talk about it. *What Should We Do About Jim?* we wonder as we braid each other's hair. Should we rat him out? If he knew that we knew, we could get him to do just about anything we want, Ellen points out as she rubs lotion on my legs. I confess that I am a little nervous about the whole thing. I tell Ellen I have been really stressed out lately planning my lesbian sister's bachelorette party. She is getting gay married in June to a Brazilian lingerie model.

The next day Ellen invites me over for a surprise. I am thinking she must have just closed the Rogers account, because she sounds so excited on the telephone. I stop by the store and pick up a bottle of champagne. I slip on my sensible heels and smooth my taupe hosiery. I pat my hair into place and straighten my librarian glasses. I knock on Ellen's door softly. I call out to her, but there is no answer. The front door is unlocked so I let myself in.

I call out to her again.

No answer.

I see lingerie lying everywhere. I almost turn to leave but then I realize that it is not Ellen's lingerie. She and I have always shared and traded panties, and I know about every single thong and white cotton panty that she owns. In fact we just love going shopping for panties together at expensive stores. We model them for each other and test the items for durability and elasticity.

Suddenly I hear a door open, and Ellen comes up from the basement. She is dressed for work. Her hair and makeup are impeccable. She looks stunning and severe. "Well, hello Sylvia!" she says with a smile. "Come here, I want to show you something." I wonder what the hell is going on. Is Ellen having some sort of lesbian experience that she wants me to get in on?

I start to think maybe this has nothing to do with the Rogers account. I follow Ellen down to the basement. She opens the door, and I explode with laughter. I just can't help myself.

There is a strange woman in the room. She is facing away from me, and she is dressed all in pink like some grotesque little princess. Her golden blonde tresses cascade down her shoulders, gleaming in the dim light of the basement. A sparkly crown glitters from the top of her head. I gasp. She is wearing spiked high heels and white fishnet stockings. Her waist is cinched tight with a corset. My eyes become moist. A new wave of laughter creeps up my throat. Is that a magic wand she's holding? I burst out giggling. I think about Ellen kissing this woman who dresses like the tooth fairy. I begin to feel like I am losing control of myself. I am screaming with laughter, and I just can't stop.

I look over at Ellen, and try to apologize. Was she smiling? She was! "Sylvia." she says to me, trying to maintain her composure. "I want you to meet Jenna. Jen-*na!!*" she calls out in a singsong voice. "Say hello to Sylvia!"

When Jenna turns around, I just lose it. I scream with laughter. Jenna's eyelashes are enormous and silver. Her eyebrows are plucked perfectly and are arched very high. I feel tears coming to my eyes as I bite my lip and snort.

I look at Jenna through squinted eyes. My jaw drops. Suddenly, I recognize her. It's Jim, from the office! Could it be? Jim? In a tutu?! It is! It's more than I can take. I explode with peals of laughter once again. I howl. I scream. I laugh like it is the funniest thing I have ever seen in my life. Imagine. A man in women's clothing! Can you imagine? I fall forward and clutch my stomach. I try to speak, but cannot make out any words through the laughter.

Ellen turns to me proudly. "Now we have the perfect entertainment for your sister's lesbian bachelorette party. Because guess what?" Ellen points at the tooth fairy. "Jenna is a lesbian, too!" This information starts me off into hysterics again, and after another ten minutes of laughing heartily, Ellen and I make Jenna prance daintily around the room. Ellen tells me that Jenna has been rehearsing some numbers for the party. Before I even have time to react, Gloria Gaynor's "I Will Survive" is thumping from the stereo, and Jenna begins lip syncing, masturbating, and dancing seductively around the room.

"You call that a feminine walk?" I screech. "My dog walks more femininely." More laughter. Ellen and I kiss each other on the lips and giggle.

"Are you supposed to be masturbating?" we demand. "That's not how girls masturbate, rub your clit!"

I continue to scream and laugh wildly. Tears are streaming down my face. My head is pounding. Ellen shoots me a secret look of sympathy and sits next to me. We put our arms around each other and laugh some more. We laugh and laugh as Jenna launches into Christina Aguilera's "Genie in a Bottle." We get up and take turns pinching and groping Jenna. She blushes and apologizes profusely. At one point, to everyone's surprise, I slap her right across the face, because I suspect she is looking up my skirt. Seeing her shocked expression makes me start laughing all over again.

Jenna comes all over herself, all over her cotton candy–pink tutu. Ellen and I are delighted and disgusted. I am still chuckling and commenting on the ridiculousness of Jim's appearance. "Wow, Jim." I say suddenly, shaking my head. "Seeing you in women's clothing was quite possibly one of the most shocking and hilarious things I have ever seen in my whole life." Jim smiles. "I don't think I'll ever forget it. Don't worry, your little secret is safe with me." I kiss him on the cheek, and laugh all the way up the stairs.

It isn't until I am completely out the front door of the house that I fall silent. I run into the street and flag down a cab. My vision feels blurry from the pain in my temples. I throw myself into the backseat and begin digging around in my bag. I find a bottle of water and a giant bottle of ibuprofen. I swallow three and try to direct the driver to my house. I have partially lost my voice and can barely speak.

As the driver pulls over in front of my house, my phone begins to beep and flash. I have a text message from Ellen. The message says, "He loved you. He wants to see us again. You got $300 for that, by the way. You can pick it up tomorrow." I flip my phone shut and jump out of the cab.

a s I sat on my couch clutching the beat-up throw pillow and the phone, I noticed that ten minutes had gone by. Ellen was saying something to me, but I was barely listening. She was telling me that Jim was in town, and wanted to see us again. She asked me when I would have some free time to rehearse before Sunday.

"And this time," she told me sternly, "he wants there to be more laughing. And wants you to accuse him of sleeping with your lesbian sister at her bachelorette party. Three-hundred bucks for one hour. Are you there?"

I wasn't. I was somewhere else. I was standing on the street. I was thinking about how I left my gold earring at Darren's house. From the pair I got for my birthday when I turned thirteen. I was so proud of myself for keeping them so long. Why did I wear them to his house? Why was I still wearing them at all? I should have had them locked up in a box or something. I was so upset when I lost it. Darren promised he would search for it every day, but he never found it. I'm sure it was in his bed somewhere.

Maybe I would look for his bracelet tomorrow, and mail it back. Probably not.

trick
Chris Kraus

I worked in the hustle bars owned by the Jewish Mafia in the late '70s, early '80s. The clubs thrived for a while, then closed at the dawn of the AIDS epidemic, when the New York City Department of Health shut down most of the bars, and all the gay baths.

I can't really separate my sense of the clubs from my sense of that time in my life or the city's. There was a feeling that it would always be there and go on, but then it ended abruptly. What stopped it for me wasn't AIDS—I got out before that—but the installation of a large restaurant exhaust system outside one of the two windows in my small East Village tenement flat. Prior to that, my apartment—backing onto an airshaft—had been kind of a refuge for me. Through the tiny crack between buildings, I observed the changing of weather and seasons. How quickly we adapt to our prisons. A slab of vertical sky, one or two trees, nesting sparrows.

I liked coming home from the bar in a cab around four in the morning. I'd get into bed, sometimes still in my clothes, and read myself to sleep. Cabs lined up outside the club when our shift ended—there were still a few old-fashioned Checkers—and I rode downtown in the deep quiet. Once, a cab driver told me to give him a blow job and pulled out a knife, but that was only one time. In bed, I read James Joyce, Merleau-Ponty, Djuna Barnes, all the Greek plays, and Colette. If I could fall asleep just before dawn, I could wake up at ten or eleven, not as "Sally West" but as myself, with the mysterious addition of two or three hundred dollars cash in my room.

You make me feel like dancing, dance the night away.

In retrospect, it was like resting between sessions of torture. Within this pile of cash, there were usually thirty or forty dollar bills creased in a vertical fold. These were the tips that customers inserted into my G-string (or, more often, panties—the dress code in the clubs at that time was not very exacting) while I was "dancing" (or rather, moving erratically in some modern dance Devo-esque fashion to jukebox songs). It was an era of humanist generalism, before special-ization ruled. No one had silicone implants; any tits—so long as they were attached to a mouth that cajoled men to buy outrageously priced bottles of ersatz champagne—would do. Likewise, the definition of "dancing" stayed loose. "Dancing" consisted of jiggling around on the stage to let the men know you were available for a date in the back room.

Still, these folded-up bills were a mysterious link between my life during the day, and my life three nights a week as "Sally West." I remember using these bills at delis and drug-stores and restaurants in the East Village, wondering each time if the (usually female) cashier knew by the vertical fold how I'd acquired the bill. The folded-up dollar bills were Everywhore's signifier. Any girl who'd ever danced knew.

It was 1978, and then it was 1981, '82. My life could have gone on like that for a very long time, but when the exhaust fan was installed outside the window, three feet from my bed, I could no longer come home so late and sleep undisturbed into the morning. The exhaust fan started roaring as soon as the prep cooks came in at eight. The sound scared the sparrows, and they stopped eating seeds on my fire escape. The apartment was no longer my cell. The fast movement of capital was putting an end to this dream time all over lower Manhattan. The hardware store turned into a restaurant, and Karpaty Shoes, the Eastern

European shoe store downstairs, was replaced by Bandito's, the first in a rapid succession of high-concept pig troughs that did business there.

Within months, the street was alive with ambition. The Bandito's waitresses, with their short '80s skirts and high heels, looked more convincing as sluts than I'd ever looked in the clubs. Everyone was going somewhere. This extreme movement forced you to look at yourself, where you were. Time was no longer so aboriginal. In this new atmosphere, those who just wanted to sleep no longer looked good.

Though I started out working at Adam & Eve on the Upper East Side, I soon settled into working three nights a week at the Wild West Topless Bar on West 33rd Street. Located on a seedy block near Penn Station across from a church and two doors from a trade union office, it seemed less competitive. There was an old neon sign with a pair of average-sized tits and a lasso. The Wild West was one of four or five places owned by Sy, Hy, and three other Jewish Mafia guys. Old, bald, with bellies hanging down over their belts in cheap white button-down shirts, the owners looked almost identical. Rotating between clubs to collect cash and check over the books, they otherwise kept a low profile. At the Wild West, Ray Mazzione was in charge of us girls. Ray spent about fourteen hours a day at the club. He was about thirty-two, lived in Queens, and said he was married. Ray hired and fired, figured our pay at the end of the night, and made it his business to know who was strung out, who was just chipping, whose boyfriend was beating her up, and who was giving out "action." He kept a list ranking our champagne bottle sales by the night, week, and month. Ray was everybody's best friend. The girls told him everything.

a t that time in New York, there were still actual strip clubs featuring big-name professional strippers with managers. There were "bottomless" bars that offered "hot lunch"—customers put $50 on the table to get a face full of pussy. But the Wild West didn't offer these things. The Wild West was all about hustle. While dancers were paid $12 an hour to show up and dance alternate sets, the real money was made selling bottles of ersatz champagne. For $35, a guy could buy us a split, and we'd sit next to him on a banquette for fifteen minutes. For $150, he could buy us a magnum, served in a curtained "back room." These dates lasted about half an hour. Given this framework, giving out "action"— any sexual contact that would result in a customer having an orgasm—was discouraged and obliquely punished. Because once a guy *spent*, he'd stop spending. Patiently, night after night, Ray taught us the ground rules of romance and dating. *Don't put out. Don't act like a hooker.* Because once you do, the hustle is over. And Ray was right. Because while a guy might offer you a big tip in the back room for a blow job, he might not deliver. And then who would you go to? Better to keep him back there buying champagne.

Girls who gave action were whores. They were not in control of the game. A "good" girl could keep a customer entranced out on the floor over three or four splits, and then get him to celebrate their new romance in the back room with a magnum. An even better girl could keep him back there ordering magnums until—whichever came first—the club closed at four or the line on his American Express card was exhausted. "You're artists," Ray told us. "You're showgirls."

A thin vestige of glamour surrounded the hustle—faint echoes of silvery black-and-white films, good girls gone astray in the big city, the Great Depression. "Would you buy me a drink? Then I won't have to dance the next set." Waitresses in fishnet stockings and cigarette trays uncorked bottles of ersatz champagne with a flourish while Ray ran the guy's credit card number. "Would you care to order another round for the lady?" Then Ray got on the phone to some primitive gray-market hacker to find out how much the guy had on his line. Sometimes he got the good news that the customer had an open, unlimited line on the card. This news was transmitted from Ray to the girl via the waitress, and so long as the customer stayed, that girl was Ray's special princess. Ray, at these times, was like Daddy. The system worked well, because it was so close to real heterosexual life. The toxicity of the club was not its demeaning of our "femininity" but in the putrid, despicable sense of all human nature it revealed, or engendered.

A typical night at the Wild West found Maritza on-stage, doing her floor work. At forty-five, this Dominican grandmother was well past her prime as a dancer, but that didn't stop her from grinding her cunt near a customer's face with a smile, two rhinestone pasties, and a small feather boa. Maritza was the only girl in the club with real costumes. As a professional, she was stiff competition for the rest of us junkies, aspiring writers and artists, and rock 'n' roll whores. "Look at Maritza!" Ray would say, when one of us stepped out of line or was suspected of giving out action.

Maritza knew how to turn on the charm. She was often the night's top-ranked bottle seller. No one knew much else about her. She confided in no one. While the rest of us bitched and complained and swapped the most intimate confidences, Maritza dealt only with Ray. (Though no matter how close to each other we were in the club, these friendships stopped as soon as we walked out the door. In real life, us art girls crossed rooms to avoid saying hello at parties or openings.)

Gabrielle, waitressing on her working holiday from Australia, walked briskly around pushing drinks. Tall, athletic, with long chestnut hair, she wore her fishnets and leotard like a school uniform. No one could figure out why she was here. She had no drug habit, abusive boyfriend, or illusions about being an artist. For reasons we never knew, she had chosen to share our place in hell.

Brandy was a stupid slut from the boroughs who liked to walk over and jiggle her tits just as you were closing the deal on a split with a customer. This often worked. Despite her poor conversational skills, Brandy sold lots of bottles. Mary, a pretty blonde woman from Allentown, Pennsylvania, had two kids and an unemployed husband. She caught the bus in to dance two nights a week and slept on a girlfriend's couch. Lorraine was everyone's negative role model, the girl in the ratty pink slip you didn't want to end up as. She had track marks all over her arms and cigarette burns on her legs. Susan S. (now a lawyer in Silicon Valley) had her own band.

The night shift began around 7 PM. The day girls—mostly bridge-and-tunnel types who saw this as a regular job—changed into their clothes and went home. Costumes were more or less optional. Girls danced alternate sets (six jukebox songs) and the rule was that whatever you wore over your underwear had to come off by the end of the first song. Your tits had to be bare by the end of the third, you used songs four through six to hustle some splits and do floor work.

Selling splits didn't excuse you from dancing, but you were let off the next set if you were in the back room on a magnum. Until eight or nine, the clients were straggling Long Island commuters. At the most, they'd be good for a split. Not that they didn't already know you'd use the next fifteen minutes to try and sell them a bottle. This rarely worked. Often you'd just give up and let them tell you their problems. *Listening* was a lower-grade failure than giving out action, but they were in the same class. In both cases, you'd lost control of the hustle.

The real hustle began later on in the evening. By nine or ten, we had our real customers: professional gamblers just back from Vegas, solitary furtive stockbrokers in three-piece blue suits, advertising executives, foreign businessmen, frat boys, and lawyers. Literal sex was not what these men came to the clubs for. As Ray liked to point out, they could get blown in Times Square for less than the price of a split. These men were legitimate hustlers in their own right, and I guess they got off seeing the hustle reduced to a girl's desperate bid to protect her own piece of pussy. Keeping a customer ordering magnums was vastly more difficult than giving a hand job. For a hand job, you just closed your eyes and took out a Kleenex, but you had to dig deep into yourself to keep the con going, keep the guy ordering magnums. My worst moment of shame came in the back room one night when I'd run out of banter. I didn't know how to talk to the guy. Unlike most of the others, he was not intelligent. Exhausted, I let him put his cock in my pussy. He left without tipping. Two nights later I had to pay Ray back my share of the bottle because he'd called AmEx and disputed the charge.

The hustle began on the table. Whenever someone gave you more than a $1 tip, you turned all attention toward him and tried to sell him a split. One split equaled $35 equaled fifteen minutes, which you devoted to selling him the next drink. It was a dream of eternal postponement. Lawyers were my special niche. They had the best sense of irony. Sitting there in my thrift-store jacket and boa with my legs spread, I was a study in cubism: lips mouthing well-bred earnest truisms about postcolonial theory, hand guiding their hand up under my skirt. And at these times, my pussy often got wet.

These are some of the songs we played on the jukebox:

"Bad Girls"

"The Tide Is High"

"Heart of Glass"

"Shame"

"Ring My Bell"

"Superfreak"

"Heaven Knows"

During the years I worked in the club, I didn't have a regular boyfriend. Outside the club I rarely had sex. For a while, a man who called himself John came in at ten once a week, bought me a magnum, and tipped me $75. In the back room, these were our dates. On our first night together, during the very first split, John said, "I have a hobby." His hobby was cunnilingus. John knelt on the floor and I lay on the couch, lifted my long lace-tiered skirt, and pretended I was pretending to come. During the day, I worked for trade unions doing theater with old people. My life at that time had become completely improbable. But at times like these, I believed.

Like everyone else who worked in the clubs, I was always trying to leave. Girls saved money, quit to travel in Europe or start their own business, then came back broke three months later. A few months after the exhaust fan went up outside my window a friend got me a job teaching college. English Composition, Greek and Roman Literature. I didn't have any degrees, claimed that my records were lost in a fire at a university 10,000 miles away in New Zealand. I taught under a false name with a false social security number so I could collect unemployment insurance under my actual name while I was teaching. Meanwhile, the college itself was defrauding the state and federal government by enrolling fictitious low-income students, then billing for tuition grant reimbursement. The idea came straight out of Gogol's *Dead Souls*, one of the books on our syllabus. Two years later, the whole thing got busted.

yeoman johnson

Juba Kalamka

Intro:

(It didn't have to be obscene

I was prepared but it's this, is it?

No enigma no dignity. Nothing classical or poetic—

Only this—a comic pornographer

and a rabble of prostitutes.)

Chorus (1x):

Just delivering a letter

Unawares as to the contents

So their slanging and their banging

Isn't hanging on your conscience

Didn't want this

You're a plot device your life a story read

That's why Rosencrantz and Guildenstern are dead

(that's what I said)

They're a party to a party

Not a clue on plans a cookin'

There's a grander scheme afoot, so look

It's right here in the hook

It's in the book it's in the paper

There's a caper just ahead

and now Rosencrantz and Guildenstern are dead

(that's what I said)

1st verse:

We've just landed on the planet

Maybe we'll get the story right tonight

Long sleeved shirt, V-neck, pants too tight

You're just a sacrifice in Roddenberry's rite of spring

The thing that keeps the story moving

Like that Klingon with the ring on

And his need to show and prove it

To the governor and king

Who've started swinging at each other

Can't kill Shatner or DeForest

So it looks like you're the tourist

Who's unlucky, ever plucky

And aware of what his fate is

This is your chance to dance, and I'm sure you've seen
the latest

In the "stop, freeze, move"

You've got the groove, and the ants in ya pants

But you don't know who you are, or who to

Or who said what/you said that, too

With a double entendre/saw vay vous, saw vay vous

And it's not your fault/but you still feel salt

In piles and the bile in your throat rises

And your breathing halts

'Cause I know you wasn't planning

to get shot out the canon

Chorus (1x)

2nd verse:

Bystanders crammed into narrative sieves

Gives the man his plans and plants a reason to live

He knows a shot in the jibs/or knife in the ribs

Contributes to why

Its takes the yeoman so much longer to die

I make you cry for the delivery guy

Write and deliberately ply

Try to stretch the limits/Couple minutes

Vomiting/ Retching

And coughing blood is cool

To catch reflections in the pools

You see it's shitty how we pity the fools

Out on a limb in film school

You're just a tool with a tool

A pen and a hammer enjambing the lines

To hide, deny that certain sway in your spine

Scream and shout/demon hollowed all her insides out

It's cheap and creepy/but We're leaving no doubt

Chorus (1x)

Bridge (8x):

Heads! Heads!

(For some it is performance; for others patronage

they are two sides of the same coin . . . or being as

there are many of us, the same side of two coins.)

3rd verse:

Yo, I'm dreading your fate

As the missile from the pistol

Whistles through the gristle in your face

And another shard of metal settles near your spine

They're holding back the SAG card until you say a line

And this is hard/but you might find

That all I rhyme was just sign in your mind

Placed there, a little space there chillin'

Will I shake spare change from the sofa, move over

The arrangement is strange and the danger is covert

It's secret we haven't leaked yet

Ain't reached the peak yet, I tweaked it

The freaks pet and the geeks vet

Get the "Goodnite Chet," and "Feel No Fret"

break no sweat and feel no pain

Reset the set and make you do it again

(the refrain?)

Chorus (2x)

Outro:

(Only inside out we do onstage

the things that are supposed to happen *off.*

Which is a kind of integrity

if you look at exit as an entrance to somewhere else.)

56

the ballad of burt starr
Michelle Tea

I'm hesitant to use Burt's name like this, publicly, in a story, but certainly he knew better than to give us, a house of whores, his true name. Didn't he?

Burt Starr didn't know us. He knew Irene, who he had sung at, that one time Goodnight, Irene while shifting in the foyer, waiting for his date. Irene was really Emily, who he didn't know. Emily, a sweet, stuffed-doll of a name, a Holly Hobbie name for this ravaged, tough woman, older and scrappy with messed-up teeth and a bunch of kids. This woman had left Emily behind. She was truly Irene to me, so I guess I knew

57

her, knew everyone, as well as Burt Starr did. As well as any of the men knew any of us.

The foyer held a sliding-door closet, and if Burt had been bored, curious, and left alone for a moment he might have placed his hand on the panel and glided it open. Inside was a dirty costume shop, the floor tumbled with stilettos, Irene's favorite shining gold dagger of a heel. There were the odd pair of dominatrix boots, should one of the many men who rang our enterprise, voices tremulous with shame and desire inquiring about the possibility of humiliation, actually book a fucking call. They didn't. They just jerked off on the telephone, straining to keep their voices even with their dicks in their hands. Eventually they betrayed themselves in a gasping gulp of a moan, and it was a race to see who could hang up first. There was a man who came through once, and I got him. Under his khakis and button-ups he wore a purple leotard, hose, and a cheap, thin belt pulled tight around his waist. He wanted me to insult him, which was easy. I lay back on the bed, clothed, and made him march in clumsy catwalks around the room. I seemed bored because I was. I mocked him a bit, and when he came on the linoleum he had to clean it up. It was a good call, easy and more interesting than the average, but when I sat at the kitchen table later the unlined fabric journal I'd bought in Chinatown open to a sheer-white page, I had nothing to say about it. I'd never be a writer. If I couldn't glean a story out of a weird scene like that I was hopeless. Empty. I collapsed on the couch with the other whores and watched talk shows through the cigarette smoke. The dominatrix boots were slumped in the far corner of the closet, unused.

The closet held a cardboard box containing a jumble of sex toys, bulbous pinks and lavenders, fleshy curves, electrical cords tangling with bits of whip. The toys, the dildos in particular, carried a toxic sheen on their skin, as if they *were* skin, sweaty skin. It was gross to behold. Nobody much used the sex-toy box.

The closet was there mostly to hang our street clothes in, and this would have been most interesting, most helpful, to Burt Starr, had he peeked, but he didn't. Irene's hoodie with her son's Hyannis High School football team logo on the front, worn with a pair of stretch pants from 1988. The pajamas Karen wore rolling into her economics classes at Harvard—flannel things marred by cute beasts, worn with run-down sneakers. Karen was tired. She ran the house and went to school full-time. She was twenty-three, an entrepreneur. You would see her in either whore clothes: a tiny black dress, cheap material, a ruffled frill, black lingerie peeking through everywhere, or these bunny pajamas. Karen was actually Penny, which was funny, Penny being a much better whore name than Karen, but where do you go from Penny. It would have to be Bambi/Candy/Brandi terrain, and Karen was the boss, after all. She needed a sensible, boss-lady name. Karen.

One wire hanger held Tanya's brown UPS uniform; the boxy shorts, the starched, button-up shirt with her name tag, Linda, pinned to the breast. Another held Rita's jeans and T-shirt. Rita's real name was Lauren or Laura, maybe Laurel.

Veronica's hanger would be of most interest to Burt Starr, as it was Veronica getting pretty in the bathroom for him, Veronica buttoning herself into a floor-length dress, all swirling flowers and gold buttons. She yanked it from the closet as Irene buzzed him in, setting the wire hangers jangling like wind chimes, and locked herself in the toilet to get ready. This was a big call, important. Veronica's street clothes swayed in the air above the sex toys: faded jeans chopped at the knee, tentacles of frayed threads dangling. A pricey Polo shirt with her initials embroidered into the cloth, MET, Mary Elizabeth Thibodeau. A baseball hat was hung backwards on the hanger's hook. Black, new, the brim still stiff. It read DYKE in hot pink letters. I had only just bought it at the gay pride parade and MaryLiz had stolen it from me. I let her. She needed it more than I did. With my short short hair and boyish body I easily read as lesbo in a way MaryLiz did not. MaryLiz's wardrobe was dull designer Connecticut good-girl clothes, her tits blowing up some girly top. Her hair was long and tawny. MaryLiz had chest cleavage, and her red pumps served up toe cleavage; if she bent over in her hundred-dollar jeans you'd get some ass cleavage as well. She needed that DYKE hat.

When Burt Starr called it was as if someone in the house had been selected for the Publishers Clearing House sweep-stakes winnings. We only had to wait and learn who the check was made out to. *Burt Starr?* Rita asked theatrically into the phone. Her eyes rolled frantically around the room, making sure we were all paying attention. We were. Okay Mr. Starr, who would you like to see today? I was frozen at the table, my pen stuck in the grip of my fist, the tips of my fingernails stabbing my soft palm. The journal below scribbled with some uninspired notes about my most recent trick, a college student from Korea. I wracked my brain, but there was nothing to say about it. Nothing to say about a fuck? How could this be. I let my pen drop.

Burt Starr.

Burt Starr? Irene whispered, stuck in her tracks, on the way to the toilet with a full bladder, her bare feet rooted to the carpet. Tanya muted the television and stubbed out her cigarette. I felt a squeeze on my shoulders; it was MaryLiz above me, spun around from the salad she'd been preparing on the countertop. Her hands were cool on my bare shoulders, damp and smelling of lettuce. Yes, Rita exhaled the word on a breath of disappointment. Veronica can see you at three. MaryLiz's squeeze on my shoulders turned violent. She hopped up and down behind me, the slap-slap of her feet the only noise in the quiet apartment.

MaryLiz was my girlfriend. She was the only one in the house whose name was a costume to me: *Veronica.* Veronica, I would purr and tease. Veronica, Share Your Soup With Me? Veronica, May I Borrow Your K-Y? Veronica, Play Scrabble With Me? Every request was a wink. Not that MaryLiz would. Share her soup, her K-Y, play a board game with me. She wasn't that kind of girlfriend. A nice one. She was the other sort. I was her first girl everything: first one she ever fucked, ever dated, ever lived with like that, in a lesbian way. Not true for me. I had more experience, but it didn't matter. I had fucked a couple of girls, been whipped into sex frenzies I liked to think were love. They had been brief affairs and I'd moved on quickly, as there was another girl on the horizon—at the bar or at the consciousness-raising rap group, on the dance floor or at the rally. But with MaryLiz I'd hit a snag. All motion ceased. She moved me into her house and now it was where I lived. She recruited me to her occupation and now it was where I worked. She slowly shut down the sex, and it was okay, had to be okay. We were women, feminist women surviving the sale of our sex all day, and if we refused each other at night it was understandable. Something wasn't right with MaryLiz, with me and MaryLiz, but our days at the whorehouse, opening up and shutting down various parts of ourselves, kept me too exhausted to look at it. Opening our crotches while shutting down our heads, keeping hearts pried open to the other workers while letting them clang shut on the johns, mediating the streams of humor and rage coursing through us. It was our job, more so than the basic sex we performed or delivered; this was the real work, this careful protecting and revealing of all our tenderest places.

Burt Starr, Burt Starr, Burt Starr, MaryLiz sang a little song as she dashed through the apartment, swooping up her make-up bag, pulling a pair of pumps from her backpack. The other girls shook their heads. Everyone was jealous. I was a little jealous, even though I knew, in my heart, that it was best he chose MaryLiz. I couldn't play Burt Starr the way she could, some crucial part of me was not tied down secure enough. A gate inside my heart would come loose and I would feel bad. I would ruin it all, I would waste the bounty that was Burt Starr. Not Mary Liz. MaryLiz was cold. She kept the phone numbers of her out calls and rang the numbers later to have little chats with their women. Your husband calls prostitutes. Uh-huh, he really does. Yes I was just fucking him in your bed on Thursday night, you have a maroon comforter with speckled red sheets, and a stack of *Cosmo*s by your toilet. She gave herpes blow jobs whenever she had an outbreak, peeling down the condom to rub the crusty sore in the corner of her lips raw on the man's cockskin. She would take Burt Starr for all he was worth, and hopefully I could come along for the ride.

I heard that he bought this one girl who worked for Marissa down on Comm Avenue a whole house, out in Newton. Not an apartment, a house! And he put her through school, Rita said, exhaling mentholated smoke into the apartment. I stood by the window, watching for Burt Starr coming up the street. Many men passed. Burt Starr looked like everyone.

Angelina? Angelica? I can't remember her name but she still drives the car he bought her. She said he's a very sweet man, Irene nodded, lighting her own Marlboro Lights 100 off Rita's smoldering stub. A very sweet man, she repeated, dreamily. I snorted. It made me crazy that any hooker would think any john could be called a very sweet man. Irene shot me a look, half glare, half hurt. That's what I heard, she insisted. Just a really nice man.

You're deluded, I said. The cigarettes were starting to look good. It had been so long since I smoked one.

You're a lesbian, Irene countered. We were finished. My perspectives on our trade were routinely dismissed because I was fucking (or whatever) MaryLiz. Because I was gay. A gay lady. The rest of them, the straight women, were playing out some ancient agreement between men and women. It was a power play, a passion play, it was timeless and complicated and exposed raw truths about each gender's base natures. I had somehow snuck my lesbo self into this scene, was a trespasser making quick cash, what did I know. They all had, or had had, husbands and boyfriends, sons. A constant of men in their lives. I was twenty-one, estranged from my family, had one male friend, a fag. Spent my time getting drunk at bars with lesbian communist organizers. I was not living in what you might call the real world.

In came Burt Starr, lingering in the hallway. He would not enter the common room, which we had straightened up for his visit, the takeout menus and general debris shoved into empty furniture cabinets. The ashtrays dumped and a can of fruity spray misted over the stink of it. Windows opened to air the place out, bringing in the traffic sounds of Boston. The television had been snapped off, and Tanya had even draped a shawl over it. A scented candle burned and a dusty, dented radio was set to classical music. All the girls sat demurely, sweetly. Rita conjured a look of seductive helplessness on her full-featured, Italian face. Burt, she husked. I mean, Mr. Starr. I'm the one who spoke to you on the phone. I gave Rita a look, lip curled. All of them hoping to swipe Burt out from under MaryLiz. All of them sitting with stockinged legs crossed, posture conscious, makeup touched up. Even Karen, who forbid call stealing in her house, beamed a gentle, needy beam in his direction. I slumped by the window in a thrift-store dress, my short short hair disheveled on my head. MaryLiz needed her wig back, had walked over and simply tore it from my scalp. I had my glasses on and could clearly see Burt Starr, who was in his fifties, maybe sixties. Gray hair and a nice suit, glasses and shiny shoes. Hello, Rita. The others introduced themselves. Goodnight, Irene, he sang, and Irene collapsed in shrill giggles.

And you? Burt asked.

Mary Elizabeth, I said. Someone gasped. That wasn't my name at all.

I don't want you taking dates with him outside the house, Karen said sternly.

Look! MaryLiz shook the heavy binder with its sheaf of schedule at the madam's chubby cheeks. Three weeks he's already scheduled with me.

See? Karen scowled suspiciously. It's not that I'm not happy for you . . .

Uh-huh, MaryLiz cut in, her mouth thin.

I am! Karen insisted. I just don't want you breaking the house rules. House rules apply for everyone, even Burt Starr.

That was the week there was a scandal at home. MaryLiz and her roommate, our roommate, had a wine party. They bought a bunch of bottles of wine and invited over friends, mostly men, all straight. The men were intrigued and delighted with MaryLiz's new lesbianism. Most of them had fucked her. They teased, flirted, passed her joints they'd rolled nimbly, their eyes stuck on her cleavage. I lingered in the back, wished for cigarettes. Wished MaryLiz wasn't such a hypocrite about vices. Pot was great to smoke, but cigarettes were poison. She'd caught me smoking one in the backyard once, pointed and laughed. Whoa you look really cool smoking your cigarette. I bet you feel really cool, do you feel real cool? What are you, thirteen? MaryLiz had a thing about alcohol, too, about beer, vodka, gin—the stuff I liked. Somehow, wine was different. Especially if you knew each bottle's origin myth, especially if you'd really laid some cash down on it, blowing much of Burt Starr's outrageous first tip. Especially if you got it at a Brookline wine shop, as opposed to a liquor store in Jamaica Plain.

After the party, MaryLiz looked in the wooden box where we kept our cash and discovered five hundred dollars missing. She screeched and hollered. She rolled wine into a thin glass, poured it purple down her throat, slammed the delicate thing down on the table. She declared one friend, Tony, the thief. Tony had gone into the room where the box was.

Everyone Did, I reminded her.

No, it was Tony.

The roommate was crestfallen. Tony was her good friend. Now she would have to hate him.

Maybe You Just Spent It, And Forgot? I asked hesitantly.

Fuck off, MaryLiz spat. Her cleavage was speckled with burgundy freckles, spilled wine.

Tony was tall and gangly, Italian, his hair a thick dark wave on his head. As far as MaryLiz's crew of straight dudes went, he wasn't so bad. Better than her ex-boyfriend, the painter, whose hair was too long and who looked right through me. Better than her other ex-boyfriend with the grown-out Mohawk and the going-nowhere punk band. Better than the upwardly mobile city planner who talked down to everyone but spoke to MaryLiz in a hushed and confidential voice. Tony wasn't so bad. He was the only one who hadn't fucked MaryLiz, who didn't hold it over me on some invisible thread. Now he was a thief and cut off. The next day MaryLiz returned with big shopping bags from Jordan Marsh, new boots, a new dress.

Wow, I said, uncomfortable.

What? she snapped. Do you know how much money I'm getting off Burt Starr?

No, I said. She hadn't told me.

Exactly. She brought the dress from the shopping bag, shook it out.

The roommate confronted Tony, who denied everything. Who was hurt and insulted and confused.

"Maybe there was a mistake? The roommate suggested hopefully.

"If I see him near this house I will call the fucking police on him, MaryLiz threatened. He didn't just steal from me, he stole from Darlene, too.

They both looked at me, expecting some emotion. The missing $500 had come from our communal fund, money we socked away for our shared, lesbian future. When we would move to someplace natural and grow food, have a baby, open an art gallery.

I woke up anxious. My guts were my alarm clock. I sat on the toilet, groggy, heaving my self out from inside myself. The sink streamed loud water to drown out my miserable sounds. Something was wrong, something was wrong. The anxiety was an energy, an electrical current swirling in my belly and tickling up and down my limbs. Every morning it was the same.

I walked back into the bedroom I shared with MaryLiz, our futon on the dusty floor. Nothing on the walls, not much in the way of furniture. Who was MaryLiz? You couldn't form a guess by a glance at her room. You would think the person hadn't fully moved in yet, that there were boxes stuffed with personality waiting to be unpacked. I crawled into bed, stirring her. What? Her eyes cracked open.

Everything's Okay? I asked. We're Okay? Everything's Okay?

Everything's fine. She rolled over, slinging an arm around me. Her voice was husky and affected, a comforting lilt and breathy tone infusing her words. Everything is totally okay. Okay?

You Love Me? The electrical tingle became a fresh hot wave, molten and thick, shame.

Of course I love you. I love you so much. Go back to sleep, okay? Stoned or half-asleep, MaryLiz could muster comfort. During the day it was different.

Burt Starr was really starting to happen. He was talking the talk, the talk he was famous for in whorehouses throughout Boston. He wanted to save Veronica. She was too good, too pure and classy, to do this work. He had feelings, real feelings, for her. Did she have them, too? He thought maybe she felt the same. He could feel it, she thought he was different from the other men. They had a connection. He had a lot of money, he could help her. He would love to help her.

MaryLiz responded in kind. She didn't like this work, wanted to get out. She had dreams, she just needed love, and support. Financial support. She had feelings for Burt, too. Burt was classy, he was kind, generous, he wasn't like the other men. She told him what he wanted to hear: The other men, they're animals. Savage. Base. They tore at her precious body, they cared not for her. Burt Starr was not like these other men. He wasn't a john, he wasn't a trick. Never mind that he hadn't had a relationship with a woman who wasn't a prostitute in his entire life. That he went through this cycle with hundreds and hundreds of girls, his finances and his capacity to be taken in by whores unfathomably deep. Yes, Veronica said. Yes, I feel the connection, too. Yes. Yes yes yes, yes to everything. She would love to be helped by him.

MaryLiz had a decision to make. Stick it out and bag the full potential of riches Burt Starr would offer. Or, play Burt Starr fast and hard and split town.

Split Town? I was alarmed.

I'm sick of Boston. Let's go, she said. I'll go first and you follow. You meet me.

Meet You Where?

Colorado. New Mexico. Arizona. I'll let you know. Don't force me to have a plan just because you can't deal with freedom.

I was stung. I could deal with freedom. I loved freedom. In fact, freedom was my favorite thing. I was so free when I had met MaryLiz—I was defending abortion clinics and getting drunk and playing Casanova with strangers in gay disco bathrooms. I was so devoted to freedom that I had become a hooker. It is, after all, just another word for nothing left to lose. Was that true? That was propaganda. What was freedom? The pulse of horrible energy that vibrated my body awake each morning? The push and clench that wrung me out, emptied me of everything.

Despite the eventual promise of a car, MaryLiz decided to play Burt hard and fast. He would place a deposit on a gorgeous, Back Bay apartment. The kind of Newbury Street brownstone where a contemporary kept lady would reside, perpetually reclining, decadently idle, in a suspended state of awaiting her sugar daddy. The place was expensive. The deposit was first, last, and security. It was a bundle. She would meet Burt at a café in Back Bay and they would do it together, like a pair of giddy newlyweds. I wondered how many times he had done this with other girls, how the girls had acted. Was MaryLiz fundamentally different than any of them? Was she more sincere, more believable? Was there anything beside Burt's own mental illness that encouraged him to believe that this time would be different?

The night before the deposit date, MaryLiz and I drank cocktails at Club Cafe. A snobby, upscale gay boy video bar. Club A-Gay, my fag friend called it. Before hooking up with MaryLiz, I would never have come to such a place. Or, rather, I would come to it for the express purpose of being obnoxious, getting kicked out. We would be underage, carrying fake IDs. We would smoke in the nonsmoking section and mock the clean gay boys in their designer clothes, we would tell them to fuck off when they stared at us too long. We would dance where there was no dancing and park it where boys were trying to get their groove going to the generic house music, standing stock-still and bored, smoking. Now I sat at a little table with MaryLiz, a plate of appetizers in the center of the brushed steel, wine for her and gin and tonic for me. I'd rather be at Jacques, the dive trans bar a few blocks away, playing Guns and Roses pinball and drinking bottles of Red Stripe while mean trans women insulted the audience in between lip-synchs of Mariah Carey. But MaryLiz hated the trans women. She thought they were misogynist and unnatural. I had persuaded her to come once, and one lady, a hefty redhead, sneered at us and called us *fish*. I'd lost. It was Club Cafe from now on.

MaryLiz's beeper beeped. It was Burt Starr. It had been Burt Starr beeping her all night long. And she had to respond, every time. It was the Eve Of. The night before the Big Day. He was feeling insecure. It had suddenly occurred to him that MaryLiz might be playing him. That MaryLiz maybe did not love him after all. I have to, Mary-Liz shrugged, flashing me the screen of her beeper with its string of now-familiar digits.

We were on a date. MaryLiz would be leaving soon, very soon, for the Southwest, some indeterminate, dusty location. She would take the entirety of the money we'd saved together, in addition to whatever she got off Burt Starr. She would use

73

it to secure a house for us, a quaint adobe with a wide porch strewn with dried chilis. At the end of the month, I would move into the whorehouse. It was temporary. We repeated these words, MaryLiz and me, Karen and me. Temporary. Just until MaryLiz found our desert dream house, and then I would be gone. I would join MaryLiz and the savings we kept in the wooden box.

Come with me, MaryLiz said. She was adequately stoned, it kept her soft. There was something in her eyes, perhaps it was love. I didn't dare ask. Nothing kills your chances for getting love like acting like you need it. I remembered who I'd been when MaryLiz had found me. A rogue in the handi-capped stall, a femme girl's opera glove balled in my mouth, her hand up my cunt. MaryLiz had walked in on us, stared a second too long, and left. It was the first incident of lesbiana she'd ever witnessed. Her gay boyfriend had brought her to the club. The femme girl left first, and I stayed behind, cleaning myself up. When I left the stall there was MaryLiz, leaning up against the tampon machine. I want to do that to you, too.

I followed MaryLiz to the bank of pay phones in the hallway. She punched Burt Starr's numbers with her finger-nails. They'd grown in when she'd stopped fucking me, like weeds overtaking a neglected lot.

Hi, she breathed into the receiver. The hallway was qui-eter, but still loud. The roar of gay boys talking and laughing, the relentless thump of their music. Burt, it's me, hi. I miss you, too. She paused, listening, a finger plugged in her other ear. Everything's fine. Her voice was husky and affected, a comforting lilt and breathy tone infusing her words. Everything is totally okay. Okay? The electricity in my body, there beneath the numb of the gin, froze. A freezing spread down my limbs and through my arms, an ice age. A glacial advance, thick and frozen and terrible, ice scraping the softness away. Of course I love you, she continued. I felt dizzy. Was she talking to me? Those were my words, my tone. I love you so much, Burt. Go back to sleep, okay?

To meet Burt Starr MaryLiz wore her wig out into the world, with a long flowered dress and her pumps. The wig looked so wiggy to me; I didn't understand how Burt believed it. Didn't he touch her head? Couldn't he see the bobby pins stabbing into the woven scalp? MaryLiz met Burt at a popular Back Bay café, and sat, for twenty nerve-wracked minutes, across from Tony the accused thief, who was having a coffee with a couple other guys MaryLiz knew. Again and again their eyes scanned over her, and looked away. Again and again they failed to recognize her, and she sat, clenched in fear of their next glance, the eventual MaryLiz? Is that you? They would laugh at her wig and make to pull it off. They would gesture at Burt and ask, Is this your father? MaryLiz was so nervous, Burt had to inquire.

Just excited, she said weakly, with a smile. They left the café unrecognized. Burt paid in cash, put the flat in Veronica's name. MaryLiz froze. Would that be a problem? It was too late now to tell Burt Starr she'd lied about her name. She had assured him she was the rare whore who kept her real name. I don't like to lie, she'd said, swelling his heart with love. It would have to be Veronica. He gave her the receipt, a gesture of trust.

Nonrefundable after this weekend, the property manager said. MaryLiz slid the paper into her purse. They lunched at the Ritz Carlton and made plans to shop for furniture. He handed her money for the meantime, for odds and ends she might need. It went in the purse with the receipt.

The next day MaryLiz wore the same blonde wig and a different floral dress back to the apartment. She got the money back. The property manager didn't want to give it, but he did. She wore him down with sweetness and threats. MaryLiz was high with it, mania shot from her face. She loaded the car. Together we lugged a trunk, heavy with all her clothes, into the street. The wooden box with our savings went into the glove box. MaryLiz was regretful. She looked at me, her lip caught in her teeth. I should've waited for the car, she said. He bought that girl that Tanya knows a Ferrari. She lunged at me, hitting my cheek with a sudden kiss. Come on, she said. Snap out of it. I'll call you from the road. Okay?

I nodded. Who knows where we'll live. It's exciting, isn't it? Her car left the street, its backside heavy with the weight of all her things.

That night I packed up the rest of the room, what was left over, my things. There wasn't much. It fit in a medium-sized duffel bag. My records, mostly new-wave British and goth-core bands from the last decade, would be left in the basement. The Vietnam vet who lived upstairs would eventually find them and sell them, same with the books I left behind. I ate oatmeal for dinner and flipped through the roommate's staticky television. I settled on *Oprah*. Her guests were two women who had been swindled by men they'd dated, professional con men.

How did it feel to learn that he was wanted by the law for having done this to other women? Oprah asked.

Horrible, the woman sputtered. Oprah handed her a tissue. I shut off the TV.

At work Burt Starr was ringing the phone off the hook. Apparently, MaryLiz had called him from the road. She had told him she was a lesbian and told him to fuck off. Burt was crazed; it had happened again. A lesbian! he howled into the phone. He was outraged. He wanted to report us to someone, but there was no one who could help him. He'd been swindled by a prostitute. Again. She should not even have been allowed to work there! He screamed in my ear.

Lesbians should not be allowed to work there! That's un-ethical! You are misleading your clients! I laughed at him. It shut him right up. Are you laughing? He puffed. Are you laughing at me?

You're deluded, I told him. The girls in the room with me gaped.

Pardon me?

Delusional, I said. You're delusional. They would tell Karen, and she would be furious. She would fire me and not let me sleep in the rooms at night, but I didn't care. MaryLiz would be calling for me any minute. I would meet her in the desert, and we would sit on our long clay porch and drink wine. The chili peppers would rattle in the gentle wind, and the sun would set orange and purple above our heads.

devices: a short play
Naima Lowe

Characters

JOE: middle-aged, hairy, fat, with a husky voice and a great love for marijuana

MARILYN: twenties, soft, fat, smooth brown skin, with a sultry young voice and hips that swing for effect

Scenes

PROLOGUE: The space between then and now, made from voices

THE BEGINNING: Along a hotel hallway, anticipatory anxiety

THE MIDDLE: In a cheap hotel room, a space inhabited by very little emotion

THE END: In a cheap hotel room, a space inhabited by an uncommon type of desire

EPILOGUE: The space between now and then, made from voices

Prologue

(In a blackout, a recorded message on a cell phone is heard.)

JOE. Marilyn, this is Joe. I'm here. It's the Bayside Inn, 135 Bayside Drive, Chelmsford, MA, Room 150. One, five, zero. The name is Joe Trillo.

MARILYN. *(Still in darkness.)* Fuck, what was that? *(Buttons are pushed and the recording is heard again.)*

The Beginning

(In darkness, the sound of footsteps along a very long carpeted corridor)

MARILYN. 112, 113 . . . Uhhh, no, the other way. 123, 124 . . . *(more footsteps, first going faster, and then slowing down.)* 147, 148, 149 . . . Well . . . *(She takes deep breaths, and then knocks on the door. The sounds of the door opening.)* Hi, I'm Marilyn.

JOE. I'm Joe, good to finally meet you.

The Middle

(Lights up on Marilyn and Joe naked in a motel room bed. Joe looks tired, sweating and breathing hard a little bit. He starts rolling a joint.)

JOE. Not bad for an old guy. You came right?

MARILYN. Uh-huh.

JOE. I thought so. Want to smoke?

MARILYN. No thanks, I have to drive.

JOE. Where you gotta drive to?

MARILYN. I'm going to meet some friends in a little while.

JOE. Your friends cute like you?

MARILYN. No one's cute like me.

JOE. Baby, this is one hell of a first date isn't it?

MARILYN. Yeah, it's great.

JOE. You sure you don't want to hang around for Chinese food? I got pork friend rice.

MARILYN. I'm really not hungry. I had fish and chips—

JOE. Fish and chips.

MARILYN. I had fish and chips earlier. Not very healthy, but very tasty.

JOE. Skinny people die too.

MARILYN. (laughs) They do.

JOE. Do you want to watch a little TV?

MARILYN. It's already on.

JOE. I've been watching a little porn-ography.

MARILYN. I see.

JOE. I hope you don't mind me watching a little porn-ography.

MARILYN. Not at all.

JOE. It's soft-core. Figured you wouldn't be o-ffended.

MARILYN. That's soft-core?

JOE.They don't show any cum. C'mon baby, watch the TV for me.

(Marilyn and Joe watch the TV. Joe is stoned and entranced. Marilyn is bored.)

MARILYN. It's less fun with the sound off.

JOE. You like porn-ography?

MARILYN. I like it with the sound on.

JOE. Most women don't like porn-ography.

MARILYN. I'm special.

JOE. *(Grabs her hand, squeezes it and kisses it.)* Yes you are. And so beautiful.

MARILYN. *(Freeing her hand, yawns)* Good thing I didn't smoke. I'd be asleep by now.

JOE. We can have a nap.

MARILYN. Whatever you want.

JOE. You could take a nap or you could stay over or something.

MARILYN. I've got to meet my friends. I have to be out of here by 10, no later.

JOE. I'm gonna stay the night I think.

MARILYN. I've got to drive all the way home. It's almost thirty minutes away. You live around here, so it's easy for you.

JOE. Actually I have a one and a half hour drive. And when I got here, I was wondering, is she gonna call me back, or should I just stay here or is she just going to show up at 8:30, and I figured you would just show up and I was right.

MARILYN. You were right.

JOE. I knew we would get along good, this would be a good first date.

MARILYN. I knew too Joe.

JOE. Could you call me Daddy?

MARILYN. Ummm.

JOE. You called me Daddy in the emails, and I like that.

MARILYN. Well.

JOE. It's just that you sound so good when you talk and I bet I'd like the way you sound when you say that.

MARILYN. It probably wouldn't seem so strange if you weren't actually old enough to be my father.

JOE. I'm not so bad for an old man.

MARILYN. But I don't think I can call you Daddy. I don't think I'd like that. You can call me baby all you want though.

JOE. Okay baby. But you got that real sweet voice. I like the way you sound.

MARILYN. Thanks . . . Daddy. Just once to be nice, but that's it.

83

JOE. You're welcome baby. I think I want to take a nap.

MARILYN. Sure, whatever you want. *(They lie down and snuggle up together. Awkward, but affectionate. Joe rubs her face and back a lot. He tucks her into the covers.)* You're not a cop are you? I guess I should have asked you that before. I'm new at this.

The End

(There's darkness, in the darkness there are the sounds of sheets and covers rustling. Marilyn and Joe settling in and getting comfortable. After a short while, Marilyn's very quiet, then increasingly loud and breathy moans as Joe brings her to a very real orgasm. Joe doesn't speak at all, or make any noise. Marilyn seems to be holding herself back at first, and then cannot help herself.)

Epilogue

(Still in darkness, with TV flickering from offstage. A car pulling up and stopping, emergency brake going up, radio going off. The sound of cell phone numbers dialing and Marilyn's message, "Hi, you've reached Marilyn, leave a message."

JOE. Hi, this is Joe. Joe Trillo, from before. I'm just calling to make sure you had a safe ride home. It was pretty foggy out there. I decided to stay the night here, about to fall asleep. I wish you were here. I had a great time, you know. Maybe next time you could spend the night with me. I could get us some food and I'd go up to maybe 300 or something if you wanted. I could get some drinks or something too if you wanted. Whatever. Just let me know if it's best to call you or email you or whatever. Okay, sleep well baby.

staged
Janelle Galazia

Pulling myself onstage, filthy club, nobody in it but some random guy rolling cigarette after cigarette with a rolling machine. Who knows why. They let you dance to the sad songs when nobody's here. The sound of Kris Kristofferson's voice croaks, and my sternum vibrates and through the other speaker a tambourine jangles. Like an alarm clock, not in the sense of being annoying but being distinct and sharply lucid like the first thing you hear in the morning. Gorgeous. Who would carpet a stage in a strip club I don't know. My heel catches on the scabby blue dentist office carpet as I begin to dance, but it does not interrupt my grace. What is the point of telling you that the carpet is scabby, or blue? What would be the point of telling you that not all of the torn bucket chairs match and that many limp on uneven legs? Are you picturing the other girls draped in the corner bored, waiting? Smoking? It sounds romantic. I feel romantic. I think I'm in love with you.

perhaps the most depressing thing about how working in the sex trade causes other women to see you as an adversary, as antifeminist, is that there is a way in which the whole thing has nothing to do with feminism. It's about money. The older I get, the more I think most things are. At age nineteen I had already been an active member of the workforce for eight years, and college was about as accessible as Mars. Looking ahead and seeing that my future was just going to be my $3.15 an hour food-service job writ large, a certain kind of occupational existentialism became attractive. It wasn't just attractive, it was practical, it was survival, it was intelligent. Sex work is not only a means to an end, it's a means to a *different* end. Given the choice between the indignity of handing people burgers for minimum wage or the indignity of showing your tits for $500 a night, the answer seems obvious. It's a choice many people will never find themselves in the position of having to make, and their insistence on trying to make it for others is totally boring.

87

The mirrors in a semicircle behind me give me six, eight, twelve reflections of myself to gawk at. I look good. Sort of. It doesn't matter, I'm a missile of white light. I'm a sword, completely washable. My movements are pretty much like everyone else's, though in my mind I can see my spine and it twists, segmented, like one of those roller coasters that loops upside down. There have been many nights like this one, and it is as ordinary as the numbered days spent in a classroom, each grade in school. Factual. Who cares?

With a few notable exceptions, people do not get into the sex industry for reasons that have anything to do with desire for sex, any more than a person enters janitorial work out of a love for cleaning. The exchange between worker and customer is a complicated negotiation of need, illusion, denial, boundaries, and specific neuroses; but central to the exchange is cash. By keeping the debate about sex work focused on *sex*, and not *work*, the true nature of the issue is obscured. The arguments rage around ideas of obscenity, appropriate and inappropriate sexualities, representations of femininity, notions of morality: Important issues in their own right, but in the context of the sex work debate they function more as a smoke screen that keeps us from confronting what's really going on. In this framework women are sluts instead of workers, or victims instead of cognizant participants in an economy. The real question here is, *why are our options so lame?* What are the economic realities that make the sex industry the most viable choice for many people?

That's where feminism comes in. That's where outrage becomes appropriate. The wage gap, welfare "reform," sexist and racist hiring practices, the decline in the real value of the minimum wage, lack of universal access to healthcare or rehab services, and the widening disparity between the rich and poor: These are the things that undermine the social fabric and degrade the status of women more than me tramping around in heels could ever hope to. We have to ask ourselves, what is so compelling about blaming naked women for their own oppression? What kinds of confrontation are women avoiding by interrogating each other rather than actual power structures?

t he club is filthy, I've said this. It is not a value, it is a fact. Factual also is the tag on my plaid schoolgirl skirt which I sweep up from the edge of the stage as the song ends. It reads Made In El Salvador. The food chain evoked by this tiny rectangular piece of information is staggering; I see the diagram of it laid out before me like a View-Master slide, bright and three-dimensional, obscuring all vision for a second and then clicking away. Factual is the beige-walled dressing room, Formica countertop and lack of privacy. I am at home here. Peacefully the linoleum peels up around the seams, fades entirely near the toilet. I pack up my makeup, waxy-smelling lipsticks. The fluorescent light hums and it is a cellular occurrence. It sings: $523, $523, $523. The club is factually filthy, but the filth is also a benevolent prop, which has been arranged by mothering hands for the purpose of me arriving there and finding: $523.

sugar & me

Mirha-Soleil Ross

Girls don't turn me on! And I am especially not attracted to the femme types who want to swish-swish around my dick. No thank you! I don't want a pair of soft lips smearing cherry red lipstick all over my balls and I'm sorry but four high heels kicking in every direction when you're both cumming at the same time, that's irresponsible. Look at my friend Kathleen in Montreal with her last so-called "Revolutionary Femme on Femme Frenzy." They were *ten* rubbing titties and trying to 69 each other all at once on her parquet kitchen floor. . . . All she can remember is a five-inch metal-spike heel coming straight at her left eye. And that was the end of her revolution! No, no, no . . . girls don't turn me on and I am especially not attracted to femmes.

At least, that's what I kept repeating to myself as I sat on the throne that night desperately trying to shit a log or two in preparation for my four-hour shift. I'd been working as a model for over two months at Cybersluts, a sleazy Internet porn site owned and operated by fags that provides encounters of the first, second, and third kinds to thousands of horny men every day.

My job at Cybersluts was quite mundane: Stroke my little baby dill with one hand while providing a few—*kitchic, kitchic, kitchic*—ecstatic keyboard interjections with the other, and every ten minutes or so shove something up my butt—a finger, a bingo marker, just about anything to spice up my worldwide affairs.

And that explains my valiant efforts on the toilet. Guys didn't like to spend $1.99 a minute to watch fingers covered in shit coming out of my ass so Be Prepared was my work motto. But on that night, I just couldn't concentrate on the deed. My hands were shaking, my feet tapping, my lips twitching, and even more revealing, my nostril wings were moving to the beat of Whitney Houston's "Heartbreak Hotel."

I tried to calm down, tried to reassure myself that this was just a momentary feeling, that it would go away as soon as I returned to the chat room, as soon as I'd take just *one* little moment to fully inspect that suspicious woman who had just struck me so intensely. I'll check her nails, I told myself. I was too disoriented to notice earlier but for sure she's got some of those long acrylic ones with French manicure that all the girls around the joint are getting and *that*, without a doubt, would make me lose my crush in a flash. I was agonizing on the toilet, still unable to shit anything more than a Glosette raisin so I figured I should just try again later and "Allez-Hop!" back to the chat room.

Sugar was her name. She'd just finished her shift and was slowly packing up. Still naked except for some red-hot lacy panties, she was taking forever to put her clothes back on. I was too rushed to let my hormones fully get in the way but I nonetheless couldn't resist taking a second look at her: Petite, femme, and delicate, she was a stunning piece of wonder woman with no less than eight hard inches of thick silver heel.

You can imagine I was pretty scattered trying to attach my garter, my transparent bra, struggling to get into my fishnet stockings and frilly baby doll all at once. "You've been working here for two months. I'm surprised we haven't crossed each other," she said while finally putting on her jeans but with this sexy black tank top featuring a red chili pepper with the inviting line Eat Me!

93

The conversation from there went on and rapidly evolved from the personal to the political. We complained about Sandy Bitch, an older drag queen working our chat room who was famous for her show, which consisted of sticking a 14-inch by 5-inch dildo all the way up her ass. Sugar and I talked about how her anal acrobatics made work for us more difficult, made us have to deal with obnoxious men coming into our room, requesting *we* too shove gigantic dildos up our ass. We wondered if Sandy Bitch realized there were no advantages for her to engage in such spectacular acts, that she would still get paid the same amount as us, $25 an hour, and that there were no awards given annually to the Most Dilated Drag Queen Asshole in Cyberspace.

I was already half an hour through my shift, and we were still bitching and bitching and bitching and getting closer. . . . A customer who went by the screen name of Mister Big noticed my lips were moving and asked if there was a party going on. "No," I said, "but Sugar is here and she's really, really pretty!" Well, I should have expected the obvious to follow "Hey, why don't you girls give us a show?" and before I even had the time to die, a very excited Sugar grabbed me by the arm, started to jump up and down screaming "Oh yes, yes, yes, Janou! Let's do a girlie show!" What could I say? "No, I am not attracted to femmes!" while

I have pre-cum flooding through my G-string? "Okay," I said, trying to look professional and in control, "but first I need a stiffener so you go get me a root beer!"

Well fuck the pop! There was only one thing on my mind when she came back in the room and you can be sure *en Tabarnak* it was her ass! She probably had some plans along the same lines 'cause she pulled this black velvet blanket out of her satchel, spread it on the couch, and lay down on her stomach with her big bum sticking up like Mount Royal.

I didn't want to act like a dog and bite in right away so I started out cute by giving her a few nice, sweet, and gentle kisses on the neck. Oooooh, she liked that! Shivering skin, dramatic spasms, her spine moving like a snake, everything that's always turned me right off in a girl was now turning me right on. And Sugar was such a girl that in comparison I felt like a big sweaty, clumsy, goofy football player.

Eventually it got time to show some serious initiative and my true assets. I have a tiny wee-wee but I got quite a nose. If you don't feel anything when I got my nose up your ass, then it's time you get a new one 'cause it's dead! So I slowly slid my nose down down down the road to the brunch. First thing I did when I got there was to give it a few discreet sniffs, just to make sure. When I got the okay from the olfactory nerves, then I started licking her up and down the crack. And let me tell you that I didn't have to say,

"Sésame Ouvre-toi!" Her cheeks opened up like automatic doors at No-Frills. I probably spent the next 15–20 minutes with my face in heaven. It was a tough gig, though, getting inside to my favorite part. *Eh Marie-Madeleine*, her hole was so tight I wondered if her shit came out like spaghetti. But once I got my tongue through . . . once I got my tongue through, it was like eating a cherry blossom except that the chocolate was inside.

Well, all good things must come to an end and at some point Sugar shot her load and said "Goodbye!" Nothing lasts forever—that's basic physics. But with every end comes a new beginning—that's paganism 101. A few minutes after Sugar left, I rushed to the washroom to finally shit my heart out. And as I sat again on the throne repeating to myself "Girls don't turn me on!" I wondered which, of the half dozen femme ones working our room, was up next on the schedule.

pimp
Tre Vasquez

I t's funny to live your whole life thinking you can do anything or be anything you want because your mami and papi in some way or another taught you that. In between their long shifts working as waitresses or cooks, eating shit with a smile for people who never worked a day in their lives, they modeled such dignity that it stuck with me. Even here now, as I recall the many effects of colonization present in my childhood, I can honor that somehow in the battle they taught me a spirit of survival that never considered death. Thank you, *familia*.

When I was seven, I dreamed of being eighteen—going to

high school, preparing for my future and going to the prom like the white girls on TV. Stupid. In reality, I'm eighteen sitting in dirty hotel rooms with men up to three times my age, pretending I'm sexy in a body that don't yet even know what sexy is. I never even went to more than a week of high school. Leaving home at fourteen, raised by the streets and by me, believing only in the protection of my dreams. I learned quick to rest with the fact that you do what you have to do.

I hate rich people. The way they look at you, the way they talk, the way they walk through the world like the whole thing belongs to them. The way they'll just about knock you off the sidewalk in the city and move up into anyone's neighborhood, yet they grab their purses tightly when you walk by and treat you like you don't belong there.

Sometime I would sit up in those rich men's houses with their marble steps feeling like any second they would realize who I really was and kick me out, afraid I'd steal their shit. Which I did, but in return they got my body for an hour or two, so I don't think they ever felt robbed. I would sit with them in restaurants, half dressed, pretending I knew what things were on the menu, knowing my only tool of power in the situation was their hard little dick under the table. I think the way I was made them feel like they were rebelling. At the same time they were correcting the way I talked, they were imagining taking me back home and how shocked and mad their parents would be. Whatever it was, I didn't really care, because I got my shit.

It got old, though . . . pretty soon I felt played out. I couldn't even find the dudes with money anymore. I never had a pimp, well, only the pimp that is working for an amerikan dream that will never quite fit in the hands of people like me. Wait, I lied. I had another pimp once, an older Italian man. He picked me up right at my front door in a Lincoln Continental one day. It didn't take me long, even being young and impressionable, to realize it didn't make sense to make your money touchin' and fuckin' nasty dick, only to have to give it back to some motherfucker whose nasty dick you have to touch and fuck too. It seemed stupid, like working for free and for what? Oh yeah, that's right, for "protection."

Let me tell you something, none of those johns ever pushed for more because they knew I wouldn't hesitate to fuck them up. I never had to tell them that. I showed every one of them by the way I wasn't afraid to look straight at them, and for whatever reason, whether fear or genuine respect, they never challenged it. See, when you tell most anyone that they have to pay for something they want hella bad, like, say . . . pussy, for instance, they'll believe you. It's about how you present the goods. If you hustle like you believe your shit is gold, they'll believe it too. If you look them deep in the eye like you can see every inch of how bad they want it, they will melt in your hand. You know why? Because wanting things makes people feel weak. And when people feel weak for something they can somehow "obtain" they'll do anything. But, when a motherfucker can smell your hustle because they got one too, that's when you got a problem. And that's when you watch a man drive away with your dignity; still confused, only half realizing what he's just taken, but it's already too late. That's growing up though.

Fuck a pimp.

By definition: pimp n.: One who derives income from the earnings of a prostitute, usually by soliciting business.

And: prostitute (**pros**-ti-toot) n.: 1. One who solicits and accepts payment for sex acts, 2. One who sells one's abilities, talent, or name for an unworthy purpose.

Take these words by definition, thinking outside of their traditional use, and relate them to the lives of those who've never sold their body for cash. I see my family, my people, every day in the position of selling their abilities, talents, and names for unworthy purposes. And these motherfuckers sittin' up in Capitol buildings determining the future of my folks and soliciting their value are, yes, deriving income from the earnings of them. By definition, this country is the biggest pimp of 'em all. Please, next time you feel for those women on the street in that alternate reality on the other side of town, take a moment, too, for my sisters in the *maquiladoras* makin' your clothes, for my brothers picking your produce, my family washing your dishes and cleaning your house. Please take a moment for all the beautiful spirits that have been labeled criminals and thrown away into prison cells who deserve freedom. Please take a moment for all of those in the position of selling their abilities, talents, or names for an unworthy purpose—the appalling economic wealth of this country.

bella
Shoshana Von Blanckensee

It didn't end that day on the roof when it should have. Bella didn't come home for a few weeks, through Thanksgiving when I waited for her up in the hotel by the window. The following Monday a key in the door and here is Bella, dropping a big green duffle bag at her feet, looking sheepish and tired with her hair and eyes that change me. All my anger slips, my wanting shifts to the front of the line. We look at each other. I can see someone all over her, on her skin, and a new jacket that doesn't belong.

"I need my stuff and half the money and I don't want a big deal." She holds one hand with the other and looks down at her feet. Her hair falls across her forehead, and I notice how greasy it is, like she hasn't showered all week.

"Okay," I say.

But after a moment of standing by the door, she moves towards me, pulling me by the wrist onto the bed covered in clothes. "Han-nah," she whines.

"What?" I say. She doesn't say anything. "What?!" I say again louder. I feel like a kid. I want to hold her and say *mine! mine! mine!* over and over again. But suddenly my face is in her hands the way she always does and her mouth is hot and all over mine, a sinking inside of me knocks and then echoes, like rings of water extending from a sunken rock.

This will be the last time and we both know it so I'm pissed. Bella is working it like her breakthrough Hollywood role; holding my face, pulling herself over me, my T-shirt over my head, taking me by the wrist again, pushing my hand up under her skirt, pushing her underwear aside, and how she stinks from no shower and god knows who, spilling into my palm a little, rocking over me, leaning on her arms straight like crutches, her hands planted on either side of my head, her mouth open some, her two front teeth and the shiny inside of her lower lip exposed, like we were still teenagers, in the dark, in her twin bed, in Long Beach, New York. I'm angry fucking her now. Saying, *fuck, you, fuck, you,* in my brain with every push and shoving the rest of my hand inside of her too fast.

103

"**T**his is stupid," I say, worming my way out from under her. It's daylight. We're in a shitty residential hotel in San Francisco. Bella's been fucking some dummy, definitely a guy, I'm sure of it now. In over our heads is what we are. I untangle myself, pull my shirt back on, move towards the door.

"Our money's still in the jar in the closet," I tell her, swinging the door open. I walk out. The hallway sings to me because I'm leaving angry now. A high pitched electric song. Pushing the fire door open out onto Ellis and charging in any open direction. I tell myself to never think of her again. Never ever think of her again. I need to wash my hands.

The birds swerve around tires. Gridlock on a Monday afternoon downtown. Everyone getting home to their houses and money and kids. I see a woman on a cell phone fluttering a hand over the steering wheel to explain, then smoothing her hair in the rearview mirror. I want a car to get into. I walk up Ellis, past Mason, turning to glance at the neon lit-up leg of the Chez Paree. The stupid leg that had started all this trouble in the first place, luring Bella and me in, the second week after arriving in San Francisco. The rain hadn't stopped for days and we were wandering, too close to out of cash—waiting till the last moment before making a fateful phone call home for help. But the call never happened. Huddling under an umbrella on the corner of Ellis and Mason we turned to see that leg, thick-thighed in orange light bulbs, kicking a red heel over the sidewalk below. Blurred by the rain the leg was more magic, more twinkle, more carnival than anything for miles. And we laughed a little. A double dare, her arm hooked in mine squeezing tighter.

I keep walking, past Reds, the dumb sports bar were I had propositioned Chris over a gin and tonic, past the Thai food restaurant with the long wooden bar to sit at, the cook rolling noodles and shrimp into the air from a giant pan. There's mayhem on the sidewalk in front of me, a man in light blue jeans is shoving a homeless guy with two hands, real hard against his shoulders so he stumbles, catches himself and then barrels forward to shove him back. They're both screaming "Motherfucker! You motherfucker!" at the top of their lungs. A woman in a too-big 49ers windbreaker is gathering all the stuff she was selling—men's shoes, a bent-up package of batteries, a stack of records—raising her eyebrows up high and saying to no one in particular, "Ho-ly shit! Ho-ly shit!" I make eye contact with no one. I maneuver my way through the three of them and keep walking. Ahead of me I see a bar. Nana Jimbo's Lounge in pink cursive. And then I see a queen with big shoulders and a curly red wig cross the street and disappear under the sign. A gay bar? I pick up the pace, suddenly with a destination in sight, make a quick dart in front of a cab, past a sprinkling of boys outside of the liquor store and tuck into Nana Jimbo's with my hands in my pockets, my eyes adjusting to the dark.

Nana Jimbo's is a long skinny place, like most small businesses in the Tenderloin. A popcorn machine with red plastic baskets and then a long wooden bar extending down the left side. The right side with just room enough for some stools against a mirrored wall and at the end of the bar, the smallest stage I've ever seen painted black and no larger then a full size mattress. A beefy bartender with a sweet coarse face and a gray ponytail serves drinks to the queen who has just arrived and an old guy with a round back, his face almost touching the bar, and now me—sliding into a stool, pushing a red basket of popcorn onto the bar, and ordering a gin and tonic. I suck it down and order another one, eat with my hand that smells like Bella.

t he hours run by as people filter in and out. Turns out the big beefy bartender *is* Nana Jimbo, which I find out pretty quickly because everyone who comes in here knows him by name. I also find out they have a poorly attended drag show every night of the week. I suddenly recognize two of the girls from around my neighborhood, under a spotlight that erases all the sad right off of them, making them smooth and sweet and brand new. It feels a lot like the Chez Paree, the magical way that a stage underneath you and a spotlight on you and a sweet strong song can change you. It had washed the thick-skinned junkie look right off of Lexi's face. It had turned Bella's hair more shiny, her eyes more green, and I'm sure it did something to me too.

At Nana Jimbo's I hand dollar bills to the girls that get the least tips. The thicker girls, with big arms and rough faces, the ones that don't pass, or have teeth that seem haphazardly placed. Then the MC announces, "Next we have the mesmerizing hypnotizing age defying wonder of wonders Nicki Delovely!" All the lights in the entire place turn off with the help of Jimbo who flips a switch behind the bar and then a spotlight comes up on the back of her, her brunette wig falling around her shoulders and a fully sequined dress with a matching shawl throws glittery light in my eyes and all over the walls. It's a song I know real well. "Total Eclipse of The Heart." Bella and I sang it over and over in the van on our way out to California, rewinding it to hear it again on the mix tape labeled Out the Door in '94. Bella had made us this tape, decorated the case with heart stickers, pushed it into the back pocket of my jeans while she pressed her lips against my cheek when I came to pick her up that very first day.

Nicki Delovely turns slowly towards the audience with big wet eyes and all this intensity, and I realize suddenly how old she is. Like late sixties or early seventies, but her eyes are wet and sparkly and she dances like a snake smooth and easy, then lurching forward with her hips every few moments to fly down the length of the bar, do an oozy turn, throw her arms up and dance her way back to the stage. She's got her eyes on me. Every time she dances her eyes land on me. When she does "Witchy Woman," she sings right into my face, flicking her foot onto my knee in a way that says, look at my panties and come on, crack a smile rugrat. I do crack a smile, but she must see the me way inside of here, how lost it feels.

a t two in the morning the bar was closing and I was officially near sick on too much popcorn and too many gin and tonics. Nicki was wearing a fur coat and a purple scarf instead of a wig and carrying a suitcase with some blonde hair poking out of the corner. She stops in front of me, letting the suitcase drop to the floor.

"What's your problem?" she asks.

I stretch my arm flat across the bar and lay my head on it. I feel shy. How do I answer a question like that?

"I don't want to go home."

She smiles at me and rolls her eyes, in a way that breaks my face, makes me smile right back.

"Where's home?"

"The Ellis Street Hotel."

"Well I wouldn't want to go back there either. You having girlfriend problems?"

I blush. Surprised she hadn't said boyfriend.

"Kind of," I say.

She keeps smiling at me and I keep smiling at her. She taps her foot a few times, so I look down and see she's wearing Keds. Really white ones, on surprisingly small feet.

"Come on," she hands me her suitcase, "but you have to pay for the cab." I stand up quickly, confused, grabbing her suitcase with two hands as she moves towards the door. She throws her hand up, tosses out a "Bye now Jimbo," pushes the door open and spills us onto the dark street.

As I wobble behind her, holding her suitcase across my chest I go over the facts to make sure. She's in her seventies, right? Or at least late sixties. She isn't hitting on me right? She's a tranny lady and how many tranny ladies really want to fuck twenty-year-old girls. Fuck girls half their age. Not even half, a quarter of their age, or a third or something like that. My eyes are bleary, and I put out my hand for a cab.

When we get out of the cab I follow her into the front hall of a giant apartment complex, the walls are white with fluorescent strip lights on the high ceiling above. It has a real clinical feel especially because I have to sign my name in a guest book and read the time off a giant clock behind the desk attendant and then record it next to my name, a huge feat for someone in my state.

Once we're in the closed elevator I ask, "Where are we?"

"We're in my apartment building, where do you think?"

"What kind of apartment building do you live in?"

"HIV positive section 8 housing, if you have to ask, but you can call it the International House of Pancakes."

I think about it for a minute.

"Does that make you a pancake Nicki?"

"I guess it does."

We don't turn towards each other but I am laughing a little and I can see out of the corner of my eye, where Nicki is blurry and tired, I can see her smiling too, shaking her head from side to side like she's sick of me already. We're both quiet again for a moment until I get up enough nerve to ask.

"Why are you letting me stay with you? "

She turns to me, maybe surprised, "I take in stray pups all the time," she says.

"Oh" I say, when I really mean *thank you* or *why?*

"Don't worry honey, I'm going to kick you right out in the morning."

I smile, squeeze her suitcase tighter against my chest.

"You think I'm kidding, but I'm no-ot," she sings at me.

Nicki sets me up on the couch in the living room, which is also the bedroom, but divided by a bookshelf that's open on both sides. She has a seventeen-year-old cat named Alf, because *Alf* was a big hit when she got him and "Alf ate cats," she explains. Alf is thrilled to have the company. She throws an open sleeping bag over me and then puts Alf on top, a real bowling ball of a cat, pinning me down, pushing me into sleep.

When Bella and I were swimming in the quarries outside of Boston, still fresh from home, I pulled myself out of the water and onto a dry rock, which was warm and perfect in every way. I lay on my belly, my head turned to one side so I could watch Bella swim around, about forty feet out. She was swimming away from me, her hair dry and fuzzy on top, then clumping into wet columns that disappeared under the surface around her neck. As she swam away the back of her little head bobbing side to side out there made me laugh out loud, and because my right ear was pressed against the hot rock and my left ear was full of water, the laugh was louder. Inside of myself. Private here with no one around. *I love her*, I thought, comparing the size of her head to my thumbnail, blurry, held a few inches from my face.

In the morning I wake up early, the way alcohol can race in your blood all night, give you crazy dreams, snap you in and out of sleep. When I wake Nicki is still asleep, snoring quietly in a big bed behind the bookshelf, I peek at her through it. She's not wearing a scarf or a wig or anything at all, and I'm surprised to see a full head of long gray hair, a soft face with no makeup so I can barely recognize her from the night before. Alf has jumped ship in the middle of the night and is curled in a perfect fluffy circle on a pillow next to Nicki's head. I fold the sleeping bag up and stack it with the pillow on the couch, then look around a little.

Nicki's apartment is wall-to-wall photos, each in their own little frame. I step closer and peer into one:

An old black-and-white photo of two queens, neither one Nicki. Matching white dresses with tan thighs exposed, the photo cutting them off at the knee. Black eyeliner, wicking up at the corner of each eye and matching brunette wigs flipping up at their shoulders. One of them leans towards the camera laughing with her hands on her hips, while the other leans back with her eyes big and soft and her chin up, her hands tucked behind her back. Behind them is out of focus, the window of a liquor store and inside, the blurry face of a man smiling with big white teeth, his hand perched in the air next to his head, palm open, fingers splayed.

I move over to another one, a color photo from the '70s, the colors faded out to orangey-yellows and browns. It's taken at the head of the table on Thanksgiving I think, a giant shiny brown turkey planted square in the middle. I see Nicki way down on the far right, wearing a blonde wig with long

Shoshana
Von Blanckensee

curly black eyelashes. All the other girls pose carefully, but Nicki has her thumbs in her ears, her fingers dancing around on either side of her head, her tongue sticking out. When I laugh out loud I hear Nicki move around in her bed. I see her lift her head and look at me through the bookshelf.

"Okay, out you go," she puts her head back down on the pillow and gestures, a run-along-now gesture with one hand.

"I was just looking at your pictures," I say.

"Honey, it's too early for a picture show, now let yourself out before I get mean." Alf stands up, stretches his back way up high, and looks at me like *you better leave now*. I mouth goodbye to him, close the door as quietly as I can behind me.

b ut two days later when I show up at Nana Jimbo's, Nicki is nonstop teasing me, shaking her finger and saying stuff like, "Where have you been Hannah-Rosanna-Dana? You think you can just leave your old granny sitting in a wheelchair for days on end while you run around town?"

And this is how it started. First we were hanging out once a week, then twice a week, and then I found myself over at her house every other day or so. In the afternoon I would call her to see what she wanted for dinner, then I would go to Safeway for the evening's groceries, pick up any prescriptions she had waiting, and a little present like a mini nail polish set, or a shiny balloon on a stick that said

Happy Birthday! or Congratulations! and then I'd show up at her door. She would open it in a bathrobe with her hand on her hip, give me a half smile and a "you again?" But she was always thrilled with her presents. She lined all the nail polishes up by color on top of the TV and was beginning a balloon collection by the window, keeping them until they were hovering, wilted, a foot or so off the ground. After she celebrated the gift of the evening, I'd cook dinner for the two of us while she watched *Cops*, Alf rolling around on his back on the linoleum floor under my feet. After dinner we'd smoke her bright green medical marijuana and she'd school me on old films from her collection of home-recorded VHS tapes. Sometimes her other friends would come over too. Like Paul, a real young performer from Nana Jimbo's, who was a boy most of the time. There was also Babette, this crazy girl from Brooklyn, real girly and small but with a voice that gave her away. I started walking Nicki through the Tenderloin to Nana Jimbo's on the nights she performed. It didn't feel safe to let her go alone which seemed to really insult her when I would even allude to it. She would roll her eyes with her hands on her hips. Say stuff like, "Hannah? Who do you think you are, saying this to me when you're just a child? I've walked on every street in this city since before you were ever born." She'd say, "If I was gonna get killed on the street, somebody would have done it when I was young and pretty,

bella   **114**   Shoshana
Von Blanckensee

not old and tired!" Nicki told me she wore slip-on heels so she could slide one off quickly and nail anyone that dared. I had seen this happen at the Chez Paree. One night when I was in a lap dance I heard a girl screaming angry from somewhere down the hall. I jumped up and pulled the curtain back and saw Lexie, Doni, and Angel running in that direction. And then the brawl spilled out from behind the curtain, four girls total now, heels in hand, raining down on a big guy who was curled into a little ball. The kind of ball they teach you to do under your desk at school if a nuclear weapon should come your way. The kind of position that could never ever save you.

One night when it was just the two of us we passed a joint back and forth after dinner, our plates on the coffee table, empty and stained with red sauce from the lasagna I had made. We were watching *Whatever Happened to Baby Jane?*, one of Nicki's favorites. She kept hitting my knee and saying, "Pay attention Hannah, this is the best part!" Then it would be the creepiest, weirdest scene ever. Like when Bette Davis dances around with a big bow on her head, holding a doll in the dark living room. Nicki would laugh and laugh and I'd end up laughing too mostly because it was funny to see Nicki laughing so hard. Laughing till tears came out of her eyes and she had to cough into a napkin.

When it was over we sat in silence for while, then Nicki turned to me, said, "You know Joan Crawford used to beat her children with a hairbrush."

I looked over at her, she was nodding with her eyebrows raised up high, her skinny hand running over Alf's back.

"I hope you never beat me with a hairbrush," I said.

"I might start." She was smiling at me so wide, and then she stuck out her hand and ruffled my hair. Like I was a dog, or a little kid, and it felt so good to be so small.

nicki turned out to be the best remedy for heartache. Every time I started to talk about Bella, even just mention her name, Nicki would snap, "Shut up! I can't hear you!" stick her fingers in her ears and sing fake opera, shaking her voice and looking up at the ceiling. It always made me forget about whatever sob story I was about to tell. It always made me laugh. It was like spring-cleaning. Sweeping Bella right out the door every time she came in.

One morning I woke up at home, stretched in bed, listened to the muffled sounds coming up from the street below, the sun cutting into my eyes as I sat up. I got dressed and ready to go eat the lumberjack special at the Pinecone Diner on Turk. I reached into the jar in the bottom drawer of the dresser and pulled all the money out. Only five twenty-dollar bills left. I sat down on the bed, holding the bills in my hand and stared out the window. I felt shocked, even though I shouldn't have been. Time away from sex work was measured in the length of my leg hair, my pubic hair, my armpit hair, and I had a good quarter inch of fur taking over. Bella had cleared out half our savings, I'd been avoiding the Chez Paree because I couldn't bear the thought of seeing her. I'd been ignoring Chris's calls for a couple of weeks, plus I'd started to spend more money, now that I had Nicki to spend it on. I peered out of the window at the street below. A gray-haired guy, teetering on legs like two twigs, was ripping up a loaf of bread and throwing it into a swarm of pigeons gathering on the steps of Saint Mary's Charitable Services. *I have to call Chris. I have to go back to the club.* I felt an impending doom deep in my gut. The pigeons were getting crazy, becoming a blur of gray wings. I was watching him swing a leg out trying to kick them back. I looked back down at the money in my hands, the doom in my gut creeping up to my throat. The apartment felt too tight around me.

I stuffed the money in my pocket, headed out, down Ellis. Eventually I found myself at Union Square standing under the statue, watching rich ladies go in and out of Tiffany & Company. Outside of Tiffany's there was a red and yellow umbrella with a hot dog stand underneath it. It reminded me of the boardwalk in Long Beach, Coney Island too. *I should save money, eat a hot dog for breakfast*, I thought. But then a sign caught my eye in the window of a tiny coffee shop a couple of doors down, a red Help Wanted scribbled on cardboard sitting behind the glass. That's when it occurred to me. It occurred to me so suddenly I might have jumped, startled. It was like a bright yellow light bulb popping up over my head. Something so obvious that I had never thought of before, I could get a regular job. I could get a regular job, like I was a regular girl. Like none of this had ever started.

I headed towards the shop, crossing through a steady current of pedestrians to tuck myself into it. I stood in the doorway blinking a little, making out a few crumb-covered tables and chairs haphazardly placed, a family of flies buzzing a tight circle in the middle of the room. I looked up at the counter. There were pastries, individually wrapped in plastic, stacked in little towers behind glass. The guy working was the only one there, too skinny, wearing sunglasses, leaning on his elbows watching me.

"What's the starting rate?" I asked.

"Minimum wage."

"What's that?"

He laughed like I was so lame for not knowing, shaking his head back and forth.

"$5.15."

"$5.15?"

Shoshana
Von Blanckensee

"$5.15."

"An hour?" I asked.

"Ya, what else would it be?"

I sat down at a table, pulled out a pen and an old receipt, and wrote on the back.

$41.20 before taxes, for the *entire* day. I looked at the guy behind the counter. He looked back at me. I wondered how he lived on that. He must sell drugs when he's not here, I thought, which suddenly explained the sunglasses. I made four or five hundred a night in the club and six hundred a night with Chris. *How lucky am I!* I worked a few nights a month instead of every single day wearing sunglasses in the fly airport, pouring coffee. I had all my days to walk around, cash in my pocket, in exchange for a few shitty nights each month.

It's so strange. The way the world can think you're nothing. That your life must really suck. When really you are so free. *I'm so free*, I thought. I looked out the window of the café, the trees shaking in the wind, shaking their shadows onto the street. People flying in every direction. From where I was sitting I could see the sky, a long column of it, blue and still, between two buildings. *I'm free*, I said to myself again, and saying it changed me, momentarily at least, like a parachute popping open over your head when you're falling so fast.

I got up and walked out, down to the pay phone on the corner, which was greasy and smelled weird so I had to hold it an inch away from my face. I called Chris, told her I was sorry for being a flake and made plans for a date that night. Then I called Nicki and left a message saying that I wouldn't be over for a few nights, that it was time to make rent.

In the evening, I took a shower and did my makeup. I scrounged around for the cleanest outfit I owned, pulled all kinds of crumpled up stuff from under the bed and the bottom of the closet in my search. I finally chose a maroon dress that came to my knees, a cardigan over it, the little black jacket Bella had bought me to arrive to work in, and black heels, normal ones, not stripper heels, so I could walk to Reds in relative peace. I stood in front of the mirror for a moment. It felt funny to be in girly clothes when I'd been out of them for a couple weeks. I pressed my hands down my dress trying to smooth the wrinkles. Looked at my face, my eyes heavy with black mascara, and my hair falling in wet curls on my shoulders. I thought of my mom for a moment by accident. How happy she'd be to see me like this. I heard her voice saying things like *my beautiful daughter*, and words like *presentable* and *proud*. It made me laugh a little, grabbing my purse and heading for the door, how in real life nothing adds up all the way.

I got there before Chris, and chatted with the bartender Lusha whom I'd befriended in a real casual way, ever since I'd begun meeting Chris there. I assumed she knew I was working, because she always stopped chatting me up the minute Chris arrived. Lusha was a very tired-looking Russian woman. I thought she was in her early fifties until a night at Reds when a big sheet cake came dancing out in Pat's arms, and the whole place was clapping and when it landed on the bar in front of her it read, Happy 39th Birthday Lusha We Love You! in green cursive. I remember looking up at her, amazed. She looked liked she'd been a sailor on a ship that chased storms, for the last one hundred years.

Chris sat down, pulled my drink out from under me and took a sip of it, her little lips squeezing around the two red straws. "Hi handsome," I said smiling. I looked at her. Her dumb fish face. Her shirt buttoned too high. I looked down at the straws in my drink. *Contaminated,* I thought. If I wouldn't kiss her then she should know better than to put her mouth on my straws. My heart started to sink a little. *I'm free, I'm free, I'm free,* I said to myself, over and over again like treading water. I got Lusha to make me another drink, and gave my contaminated one to Chris. She thought it was so sweet, like I was buying her a drink when I'd never done that before.

Chris launched into a never-ending rant about work. The department had made her take an apprentice, an especially clueless one, and I was saying comforting things. Stuff

121

like, "That sucks, Chris" and "It'll take him a while to learn, but he will." But I was just hearing myself say it.

She was so arrogant and could never stop talking. It was so annoying. Maybe her diarrhea mouth is part of the reason she can't get a real date, I thought to myself. I was fake listening, sometimes wandering with my eyes by accident, watching my hand on her knee, seeing my own legs, my heels hooked on the bottom wrung of my barstool. There was something so strange that always happened the minute Chris arrived. I'd feel fine all day and then we'd meet up and I'd die a little. Not die exactly. Float in and out of myself like I was on mushrooms when I wasn't.

When we got to her loft I just let her have it. She said "Tiiimmm-berrrrrr!" and laughed like she was so funny, as she pushed me from standing, face down onto the bed. It was rude and not funny but I didn't care. It would be easy this way. My chest against the bed instead of her. The radio was on quietly, and she'd lit a few candles while I was in the bathroom as if it would mean something. But the radio and the flames blurred and then floated away. I was sinking now, like a submarine, right into the mattress. It didn't matter what she was doing, what she was whispering to me, what I was whispering back. I was so far under water now. The blankets and pillows pulling me down like a net. My eyes closed and webs of light, like drops of paint hitting a window, would flash across my eyelids. But if I tried to focus on one, it would disappear and a spot out of clear view, to the right or left, would break open with light. And then further back from my eyes I could see the front of an aluminum boat moving gently backwards on top of the water, moving in a rocking motion. And the light was bouncing off the water and the boat so that everything would go white for a moment and then return into view. I pushed my hands down, felt the hot-ridged metal of the bench I was on. I felt my bare feet in a little puddle at the bottom of the boat, warm from the sun, and then I turned around, looking behind me. There sat my grandmother. My grandmother with a firm grasp of the oars, lifting them dripping out of the water, leaning forward and then dipping them down, again and again. This motion over and over and the light bouncing. I looked at her arms, how strong she was, and then down to her legs, free from the braces and brand new. Her legs and feet uncurled, sturdy and muscular. Then I saw her face. Her soft face, and her eyes, big and shiny, and her eyebrows smooth, not wanting anything from me. I worried for a moment that she might be angry, that somehow she must have known what I was doing with Chris, but if she did, she didn't show it. She just looked at me with all this soft love, like she was trying to row towards me even though I was there in the boat with her. The oars lifting, dripping from the water, then dipping down to pull again.

college graduate makes good as courtesan

Veronica Monet

Born to working class parents in 1960, I was taught the value of a dollar early on. I never had an allowance and considered children who did to be strange creatures from another world. In my family, everyone did their share and worked hard with their hands. One never expected to get paid for doing one's chores. My father had little use for formal education. He only went as far as the eighth grade and even seemed to possess a certain amount of contempt for book learning. On more than one occasion, he slammed my textbook shut with the following proclamation: "Put that away, I have some *real* work for you to do!" "Real work" was without fail something that would put sweat upon my brow: raking, hoeing, hammering, hauling heavy objects, etc. My childhood was this constant struggle between my simple roots and the more educated future I dreamed of. On the day I was moving out of my parent's home and into a college dormitory, my father took me aside for a father-daughter talk. He implored me to forget this silly notion of getting a college diploma and stay at home with him and my mother. He promised me that the education would be a waste of time and Uncle Sam's money (I was the recipient of government grants due to our family's low-income status). Since I was destined to marry and have children by the time I was twenty-one, I certainly didn't need an education in order to be a proper wife and mother.

My father's speech was ill-timed. The year was 1978 and the feminist movement was in full swing. I knew I did not want to be a wife or a mother. I wanted a career. I wasn't sure what I wanted a career in, but I felt certain a college education would help me get there. I majored in psychology with a minor in business administration. Much to my chagrin, there were many female students in the liberal arts school who joked that they were getting their "MRS degree." I bristled at the thought. I took my education and eventual career seriously. Maybe I would get a master's and become a counselor. Maybe I would take my bachelor of science degree into the business world and climb my way to the top of some corporate ladder. What mattered most to me was making it in a "man's world."

Upon graduation, I set about doing just that. I secured a desk job at a small telecommunications firm with the intention of working my way up. I took a myriad of on-the-job classes in everything from customer service to the installation and repair of small electronic–key phone systems. When my supervisor was fired, his phones, paperwork, and technicians were rerouted to my desk. I was in charge of everything except signing the technicians' checks. Department revenue went up considerably while I was running the department. I was elated. Surely a promotion would be forthcoming. But my reward for doing two jobs at once without a pay increase was getting to train my new supervisor. I had to tell him everything. He spent more time at my desk asking me silly questions than he did at his desk doing his job. After this humiliating experience, I surmised that my climb to the top was going to have one major obstacle: my gender.

Don't get me wrong, I didn't give up that easily. I struggled for another six years. When that job didn't lead to success, I tried another company, another position, more classes. . . . My last straight job was in 1988 as a marketing representative for a radio station. My boss would assign me accounts with the following admonition: "You take this account, Veronica, he likes a good-looking pair of legs." I hoped my sheepish smile would not give away my mixed emotions of being complimented and insulted simultaneously. My efforts to land these accounts usually ended with the potential client admitting he never intended to buy advertising time with my station; he just hoped he could talk me into going out with him. And then I remembered a rule of business from college: Never define the product for the market—let the market define the product. Maybe I was selling the wrong product. If my clients wanted me, why not give it to them? And instead of only making 10 percent commission, I could take 100 percent.

This brainstorm hit me at the same time I was dating a male stripper and a female prostitute. I doubt I would have ever made that leap in judgment had it not been for the fact that I knew real people in the sex industry, and they were people that I liked. I asked my girlfriend to teach me her profession. There was a lot to learn despite popular jokes to the contrary, and I employed almost everything I learned in college to become a successful prostitute. My mentor taught me to do things the way she had. I got a business license and began paying quarterly taxes right from the start. I learned to screen calls so I only did business with suitable clients and I learned to use latex barriers properly to protect my health.

My new career was so much more honest than the corporate world I left behind. At first I thought I was trading in sexual harassment and gender discrimination for sexual objectification that paid extremely well. The men I saw as a prostitute were no better and no worse than the men I worked for and with as a senior customer service coordinator or marketing representative. Now instead of enduring on-the-job sexual innuendo for a meager paycheck, I was paid more in one day than I used to make in a week. The sex was honest and straightforward. The money was cash up front. My pragmatism made prostitution an attractive choice.

What I did not know in 1989 when I began my career in prostitution is that it would blossom in a way that would eclipse my expectations for any career, let alone one in the sex industry. Eventually, I worked my way up from prostitution by the hour to high-end escorting and finally to being a courtesan. My clients would be some of the world's most gifted, accomplished, intelligent, and wealthy men in the world. Their generosity of spirit would touch my life in ways far more meaningful than their money. And my initial animosity toward men would be transformed to a healthy capacity for empathy and understanding that all genders are struggling against a system that demands conformity to proscribed gender roles.

I also discovered that my clients, for whatever reason, were more prone to worship women than objectify them. In the beginning, I attracted plenty of men who objectified me but as my career progressed, those superficial souls disappeared and I only shared time with substantial individuals who longed to service the goddess incarnate. They probably would not choose those words, but nevertheless their actions expressed this sentiment. I have been showered with love and gifts and money. But what has touched me the most has been the degree of vulnerability my clients have shown me. Whether grieving the death of a family member, dealing with a physical disablement or disfigurement, struggling with major life decisions or facing their own mortality, I have been honored to share the most private of thoughts and emotions. And that has lent a depth of fulfillment to my career in the sex industry that I never ever hoped for as I charted my corporate career.

I am often asked if there was ever a negative side to my life as a sex worker. Of course there was. The most difficult part of being a sex worker is dealing with society's stigma and legal sanctions. I was arrested once. That was a degrading experience, which is ironic since law enforcement claims to be attempting to "save" women like me from degradation. My arrest led to my eviction from my apartment because the laws are written so that landlords are implicated as felons unless they evict a woman accused (not convicted) of prostitution. Some so-called friends dropped me from their list of people to invite to their dinner parties. I have been accused of being the daughter of Satan by religious fanatics. Et cetera. In other words, the work is better than other work I have been paid for. But the hatred of society is hard to deal with and so most people don't.

Early in 2004, I announced my retirement from prostitution. I have a benefactor or two who will no doubt remain my friends forever. But my career aspirations are now turning to that of being an author. I can only hope that writing will be as fulfilling and fun as my fourteen years in the sex industry.

campus sluts forever! Jessica Melusine

I. BRIGHT COLLEGE DAYS

It was a regular office in an early-20th-century house in a Midwest college town, with block glass on the windows so neighbors couldn't see in, where the copier creaked out slow copies and ran low on toner and where we had smoke breaks out in the back and listened to the traffic on the main road.

"He had me going for an hour," Lola would say, and drag on her menthol cigarette while inside Tyler was explaining a particular foot fetish to the New Girl while keeping the customer on hold.

"Only tennis socks, only tennis socks or he'll get upset!" she said and pressed the button. Lola and I walked back in through the corridors and back to our respective cubes.

It was 3 AM, I pressed the button on my phone and Alexis roared back to life from inside me as my phone rang and I answered with a high-pitched, "Hello, honey, thanks for calling the Campus Sluts!" trying to mask Melanie shouting, "Take it, bitch!" to her client from the next cube. I had a credit card to run and a cheerleader call to do. It was another night at the office, another night at the Campus Sluts. We had our traditions and like sorority songs or pep rallies, they stay and stay.

II. PHYSICAL FITNESS, MENTAL FITNESS

"So, we all have a gym."

"What?" I said.

This was the story that we were supposed to feed prospective clients at the phone sex office, the ones who asked us how a bunch of horny college girls at the Large Midwestern University (all 18–23 with measurements that would make Playboy swoon and we all said the girl in the college issue worked with us anyway) got into the phone-sex business, if they even bothered to ask at all. Management never remembered to tell all of the girls so we'd adapt when we heard it. Apparently, in a story of secret, sexy origins, it started with a health club that some seniors at Large Midwestern started (we never said the name of the school, but let them wonder and draw conclusions even though most of our relations to the school were just hearing the roars from the stadium on game day). According to the story, the rent couldn't be paid on the gym so the phone-sex business started in the back. This meant that in between laps on the StairMaster and trips to the shower, we could take calls and in a hybrid of wanking and philanthropy, the client would save our gym, relieve our sexual tension, and in doing so contribute to our education at Large Midwestern. It also explained our predilection for hanging out together, presumably when we weren't all attending the same orgies.

So, we worked out together and if they "guessed" the name of Large Midwestern, we'd just giggle. It made them feel smart. Some used the gym story in addition to the college, some didn't; Lexus always liked to say she'd just gotten out of the shower, the water dripping down her long, lithe body, off her 5'9" frame and B-cup tits. She'd smile at us over the phone mouthpiece, her grey hair glinting yellowy in the overhead fluorescent lighting. It came in handy if I had been running for the phone from getting my bag meal at the fridge, breath heaving and heavy.

"Ooooh, it's the StairMaster!" I'd say, settling into the office chair with the broken wheel. "I was just getting warmed up, baby. . . . I hooked up with the cutest girl here one day . . . did I mention she was one of those wild art major girls?"

No one questioned why we were there late at night. It was finals or Greek Week or something and anyway, in my case, all my sorority sisters went there too. But they didn't know my naughty phone-sex secret since they were too busy violating pledges with Push-Up ice cream pops or, in a story that led me down a road that never ended for one client, taking them to the Large Midwestern University Medical School so they could volunteer to be examined by the young gynecology interns. It was all sorority speculums after that and he never wanted to hear about my arm curls. Others just wanted to hear about school.

"I'm worried," a client once said.

"About what?" I asked.

"That your submission to me may affect your grades."

I asked him about applying to grad school and the next time he called with advice for forty-five minutes and I was able to tell him all about my 4.0 and my goals. After that, it was time to play slave girl and blow job, and he assured me I'd be fine, just fine in grad school.

III. THE IMPORTANCE OF TRADITION

We had traditions and we had game days. We were in a college town, after all. Late nights when we spun on our creaky chairs, made slurping noises on the phone, and read and reread the same tattered issue of *Foxy Boxing*, we had a game.

There was an envelope full of words written on slips of paper. We crammed them into the envelope until it was full to bursting—and we played it like this, fast and furious. The minute one of the girls got on a call, she'd open the envelope and draw out words that had to be used in the call. We were very creative, since we had time on our hands. The player wrestled with words like gravy boat, Mrs. Beasley doll, corncob, and a variety of Ozzy Osbourne lyrics we threw in for good measure.

"Oooh baby," I'd say when it was my turn, "you're gonna make me bark at the moon." We'd all huddle around the speaker in the manager's office and howl with laughter as the player would purr, "Oh honey, I'm gonna swallow up that corncob!" followed with "I bet you wanna touch my squirrel, don't you?" and "That's right, play with Mrs. Beasley!"

Laughter would vibrate through the thin walls. Sometimes the player would have to press the mute button on our big, heavy office phones so she wouldn't laugh, wouldn't break her throaty whisper or high-pitched-giggle girl voice. The men, if they were confused, didn't show it; they just kept stroking their corncobs (or sporks, or pencils) until the end result. We wondered often if they were so drunk they didn't care or if we'd somehow reprogrammed their erotic responses.

She pulls a slip of paper and covers her mouth with her hand and in the office we take a deep breath. "You know what I hear in my head when I'm fucking?" she says to the two men on the line, each of them sharing an extension, jerking off to her voice, as close as they have ever come to touching. "War Pigs," she says, and hums it in a porno moan as we in the office giggle and applaud.

"Oh baby," one of the guys says, "that's so fuckin' hot!" and it's all over for him, it's all heavy breathing and exhaustion and we're all collapsed on the floor, trying to breathe from laughing so hard. She was the queen from then on.

It got us through the long nights, through the cavalcade of drunk calls when the bars closed on the West Coast, through the callers who just wanted to hear how much you were a no-good dirty whore, through the ones who just wanted to hear you come. Until the morning, when the sun rose and the day shift and more managers came on.

IV. SO WE COMMENCE

We had a high turnover at Campus Sluts. People graduated from the actual Large Midwestern, moved, got tired of the coprophiliac calls or had a fight with the manager, anything, and I was one of them after a year and a half. My last shift I came out as the sun came up. I'd be moving to Boston that morning and as I walked to the car, I wish I had a tassel to turn or a hat to throw. I've since worked as a model and I still work as a home-based phone-sex operator now and then and when I do, I think of the Campus Sluts and look back on those false years at Large Midwestern with a sort of pride. I did a lot: I won the English department essay contest, gangbanged the whole Sigma Chi house, applied to grad school, did my first *bukkake* film, ravaged innumerable pledges with vegetables, fingers, and frozen desserts, was intimate with balloons—all while working out every night and getting a well-deserved 4.0. If that isn't dedication, I don't know what is.

an interview with gloria lockett
Siobhan Brooks

Gloria Lockett is the former codirector of the prostitutes rights organization COYOTE (Call Off Your Old Tired Ethics) and Executive Director of the California Prostitute Education Project (CAL-PEP), an Oakland-based, nonprofit AIDS and HIV prevention organization that works with street prostitutes. Lockett served on San Francisco District Attorney Terence Hallinan's Task Force on Prostitution and as a member of former Governor George Deukmejian's California AIDS Leadership Task Force. She has been published in several anthologies, including *The Black Women's Health Book: Speaking for Ourselves*, edited by Evelyn C.

White (Seattle, WA: Seal Press, 1990), *Sex Work: Writings by Women in the Sex Industry*, edited by Frederique Delacoste and Priscilla Alexander (San Francisco, CA: Cleis Press, 1984), and *Lessons from the Damned: Queers, Whores and Junkies Respond to AIDS*, by Nancy Stoller (New York: Routledge, 1998). She was also, for eighteen years, a prostitute.

SIOBHAN: What led you into the sex industry?

GLORIA: Money. I was young, twenty-one when I first got into the sex industry. I had two jobs, one as a clerk at a Lucky's store and the other as a clerk at City Hall. I was also waitressing at the Hyatt House Restaurant and various hotels in Oakland, trying to support myself and my two kids, and it was very, very hard.

SIOBHAN: How did you begin working in the sex industry? Did you have any connections with people who were already working in it?

GLORIA: During that time women in San Francisco worked in their fur coats. They were nicely dressed, and their hair would look good. One day, I said to this guy I was seeing, jokingly, "I could do that." Next thing I know he was bringing me a black dress and telling me to put it on. Basically, he and I were going out to work. That was in 1967, and it just went on from there.

SIOBAHN: How long were you in the sex industry?

GLORIA: I still consider myself to be in the sex industry, but as far as dating and working for myself, I was in it for eighteen years. I worked on the streets for about ten years, and then I worked in clubs in Burlingame and different hotels. In the latter years I went to working ads in newspapers.

SIOBAHN: How were issues around safety and clients dealt with?

GLORIA: I was working in a stable with lots of other women for about eighteen years straight. For ten of the eighteen years, there was an average of ten of us, me being the eldest. We were always around each other and worked in pairs on the streets and in hotels. We had procedures where if you got out of a car and no one was around, you took down the guy's license plate number, or someone driving behind you took down his license number. As soon as you got into a hotel room you would pick up the phone and tell someone where you were and what time you were expected back. For the most part, I felt pretty safe; the streets are a little more dangerous than being inside, but a lot funnier. When you worked inside you had to play girlfriend and boyfriend, but on the streets the guys knew what you were down there for. They knew why they were picking you up—there were very few games that were played.

SIOBAHN: How was race an issue in terms of how much money you made?

GLORIA: The money varied. It went up and down depending upon what city and what town. Over the eighteen years I worked in a lot of different states. In order to be black and work the sex industry you had to move around a lot. In each state the money was different, anywhere from $10 to $600. I've worked Vegas, Hawaii, Alaska, Oakland, San Jose, San Francisco, and other small cities, so money depended on where you worked and what kind of date you were going to turn. If you were in Vegas in those days, the average date was $100. Most of the time the guys would offer you as little as possible. If you were on the streets they would offer you $10 or $20, but the art is to talk the men out of however much you could get instead of taking what they offered you.

There was a time when I was on the streets that I could turn as many as ten or eleven tricks a night. But if you were in a hotel it was more like three or four, and if you worked out of ads in papers then it was five or six. If you worked in Alaska prices were up in those days because of the pipeline, so men had lots of money, plus it was very cold. Guys would work three months at a time before they would be ready to spend their money.

Race played a very big part in how much money you

made. Fortunately or unfortunately, I hung around a bunch of sisters who were white. We all helped each other out. If one of the girls would catch a date, we had an apartment or checked out the pad that we were working out of. The two or three black women would wait until they got to the apartment and we would double-date. So, if you were standing out on the corner, they would definitely pick up the white girl first. No matter how big, ugly, or old she looked—it didn't matter: The white girl went first, then the black girls.

When I worked the hotel scene there were very few blacks, so you had to be very careful. You had the chance to rip guys off, not that I did, though it was tempting at times. But you couldn't rip guys off because there were only two of you, and people in the hotel would know who you were, even if the guy didn't.

You couldn't hang around with other black girls. You had to hang by yourself or with other white girls, because if you were hanging in the Fairmont or the Hyatt, the people working there were more apt to bother you if you were with another black girl. I might have hung with one black girl from time to time, but for the most part I hung with white girls or by myself. It's a very racist thing, for different reasons. Some people have never seen a black woman; they're raised in areas where they don't see black women until they're grown. Actually, I remember one time I was standing on the corner of MacArthur in San Pablo and this guy kept passing by looking at me. Finally, a stable sister of mine came out—a big white girl—and he picked her up. I waited until he got to the house; waited until she got her money. Then I went in and said to the guy, "You've got to tell me why you picked her up because I know that you were more interested in me than her. What is it?" He was shaking and he said, "Well, I didn't see a black person until I was twenty. I was too scared." [laughs] Racism plays a part in anything that you do.

SIOBAHN: Was the money more equal when you were with other black women?

GLORIA: Well, it's hard to say because the skill was not how much a person would offer you, but how much money you could talk them out of. I think it was probably about equal; of course they would give a white girl more money than they would give you. So black girls knew that they had to talk. I always figured if you had the money on you, then you should be prepared to spend it. Unfortunately, this was before ATM cards. [laughs]

SIOBAHN: How many times have you been arrested and what were the circumstances of your arrests?

GLORIA: I've been arrested about forty times. The first time I got arrested it was horrible; I was in San Francisco and a sweep happened. They arrested me and about thirty other prostitutes. I had never been to jail. I was twenty-one. I didn't know anything about jail and I didn't know anyone who had ever been to jail. I remember I was in jail crying and one of the girls whispered to me, "You can't cry because if you cry the other girls are going to talk about you."

I was like, "I don't care! I'm never going to do this again." The girl said, "Aw, baby. You'll be back out there tomorrow." She was right. [laughs]

They had you sleep on cement floors with wool blankets, which I'm allergic to. The toilets were in front of the bed, so there was no privacy. In the first year I pled guilty, so I was on probation for a year—it was horrible. After that, I fought all my cases and I have to say that I'm a little bit different from the average person because I refused to think I was a criminal. I got up every morning and went to court, and used a public defender, sometimes private lawyers. I spent a lot of time in court and—knock on wood—I never served more than three days. But it was very difficult because if you're on the streets you get arrested, you're an easy pickup.

Police always want easy marks, and prostitutes are a lot less dangerous than a domestic violence call. If you're not on the streets, for the most part, you won't get arrested. Police constantly harass prostitutes; police have arrested me and said things like, "What if we put sand in this Vaseline? That would really be something." They used to take our condoms and punch holes in them. So, the police were really bad, and that's another reason why you had to move around. I really hated it that we had to move around so much. Trying to raise kids and moving from one city to another city was hard. But my kids' lives were a little more stable. Either my mother kept them or the housekeeper did, so they weren't jumping all over the place like I was. I moved around a lot to keep from going to jail. Jail back then is the same as now, most people in jail are black. White people who go to jail don't stay and they don't get the same amount of time.

SIOBAHN: Were murders of prostitutes a big concern for you when you were working the streets?

GLORIA: It's always a concern, but my situation was a little bit different because I hung around so many people. Misery does not like company, so most of the time the women that were getting murdered hung by themselves. There was a time when pimps, if you will, would not let their women work with other women for fear that their women would become more educated and organized and leave them.

I can remember a particular woman who used to work the streets, and she and her old man were IV drug users. She had six kids and she was always by herself. One day a guy picked her up and killed her. It was really bad because she was a white girl and she was with a black man. From what I heard nobody claimed her body because her parents disowned her after she got involved with a black man—prostitution was just another factor for her parents disowning her, but racism was really the issue. Her body stayed in the morgue for thirty days. So, that was the most fear of working the streets by yourself. I think women shouldn't be by themselves; people try to take advantage of women anyway, but when women are by themselves, they're more likely to be victims.

SIOBAHN: Did you ever have a pimp?

GLORIA: Yes. I was with the guy for twenty-five years. He was the same guy that got me into prostitution. I left him a couple of times, but he was the only pimp I had.

SIOBAHN: Was the relationship good?

GLORIA: Yes, but it was hard. Any time that you have a man that has anywhere between ten and twelve other women, it's difficult. He was a very good man, which is why he had so many women. He was very likable and very family oriented, not the type that would beat you and make you stay out all night, and he didn't make you fulfill a quota. We all just thought of him as our old man rather than our pimp because he wasn't the stereotype of a pimp.

You know, wearing the hat tossed to the side, jeans, a three-quarter leather coat, and big shades.

SIOBAHN: How did your kids react to you being a prostitute?

GLORIA: It's hard to say because my kids were three and four when I got with the guy. So he was the only father that they knew. My kids starting asking me about it when they reached ten and twelve years of age, but before then it was never brought up. None of the prostitution took place around them . . . but they knew. Having housekeepers, living in fine houses, driving Rolls Royces and Cadillacs, and having a whole bunch of white women around the house: They knew.

After a while they asked. I used to just tell them I was going to work when I would leave them, then they asked me what kind of work was I doing. They were so used to having designer clothes, I don't think it affected them much when they were younger. However, I do think now that they're older [prostitution] had an effect on them which I'm not happy with. Both of them are not as stable as I would like them to be, especially my daughter. And who knows? I don't know if it's the prostitution or me not being around them when they were growing up. We love each other. Neither of my kids have said anything like, "Oh, Mom! We hate you because you was a ho."

SIOBAHN: How old are your kids now?

GLORIA: I'm fifty. My son is thirty-three, and my daughter is thirty-two.

SIOBAHN: How did you become involved with COYOTE?

GLORIA: I got involved with COYOTE because there was a group of us working the streets of Berkeley, Oakland, and San Jose. When working the streets of Berkeley, the police started to figure out that we were prostitutes all working for the same person. This happened around the same time as the Jonestown Massacre. The police would say that the guy we worked for was another Jim Jones, brainwashing us, and that they would catch him like they caught Al Capone. So the police got really heavy on us.

When we started working San Jose back in 1977, there was lots of money, until 1983. What happened was [the police] started watching us, and they set us up. One night the police called the house we were working out of. I was the one answering the phones, setting the girls up on different dates. Then they came in and busted me; I was the only black woman. Six women got busted, but two of them weren't there, so they didn't get busted. They charged me with pimping and pandering, conspiracy, 647b [which is prostitution], being in a house of prostitution, being around a house of prostitution. They charged the other [white] women with

647b. The six customers got tickets, they were never arrested, and they were made to testify against us. We spent a year in court, and according to the police, it cost the taxpayers a million dollars for a prostitution case. I refused to plead guilty to conspiracy. I told the police that I would plead guilty to being in a house of prostitution, which is six months probation, which I could deal with.

In the next bust, the police only went for me and my lover (who was black), and one other woman (who was also black). They tried to get all of the white women and the Mexicans to testify against us! It was a huge case, and they charged us with every felony there was. They charged my man with having a gun in the house. My bail was $500,000. My old man's was $1,000,000. When I got the first case, I had tried to call Margo St. James, but I didn't really follow up. But when I got the second case, we really needed some kind of help and support.

The police also asked the white girls to testify against the black girls; some of them wouldn't and stayed in jail the whole time of the trail. Margo St. James went to court with us every day. I won my case; the other woman pleaded guilty and did a year and a half. My old man got twenty years. He did two-and-a-half years and then won on appeal.

After the trial I became more involved with COYOTE. I knew that, for the most part, the people working the streets were black and other women of color. So I had a real problem with the fact that COYOTE was so white. The people were real nice, it was just too white. But I wanted to be involved with COYOTE to let my people know that prostitution was not an all-white issue.

I turned out to be quite an activist, but mainly because I knew that there had to be a voice for people who were working the streets and getting arrested—which meant mostly black people. Those were people to me who were doing prostitution big time. It was horrendous to me, the white women who would turn two tricks a month and call that prostitution, when black women were working the streets turning five and six dates a night. They were working six days a week in rain, cold, and snow. I felt it was important for me to be a part of COYOTE to let people know that black women's issues were different from white women's issues.

For the most part, white prostitutes work inside, and many of them get into prostitution because of power issues. Some were once in the professional world and felt like they were being treated like whores. Many of them have gone to college. Black women mainly do prostitution to economically survive. Most of them never had the opportunity for higher education.

I think black prostitutes think COYOTE is a waste of time. They feel that prostitution is never going to be legalized or decriminalized. Many of them feel that they don't have the time for meetings because they're too busy making money, and that the meetings aren't going to benefit them in any way. I do understand all those reasons, and if I hadn't been in the situation I was in, I probably would not have attended them, either. However, I definitely think that my being at these meetings made a difference. Though COYOTE is still mostly white, they understand many issues relating to women of color that otherwise would have not been addressed. I served for two years on Hallinan's task force to decriminalize prostitution in San Francisco, and I'm sure I made a difference by being on the task force. I've been to the International Conference on Prostitution in Amsterdam, which I also think was valuable. Black women do need to be heard.

SIOBAHN: How do you feel, overall, about your experience as a prostitute?

GLORIA: My parents are dead. I'm the oldest in the family. I'm not proud of what I've done, but I'm also not ashamed of it. I've learned from my experience, and now I have my job at CAL-PEP: California Prostitutes Education Project. If it hadn't been for my experiences as a prostitute and with COYOTE, I wouldn't be where I am now, at a place where I can talk about it and let black women know it's okay. But many people feel that the older they get, the more they want to forget about certain parts of their life. People will say, "Oh, that was back when I was on drugs," or under someone's power. I feel that my being visible and talking about my experiences will let people know—especially let black women know—that it's all right to have a past. We all have closets. So, I think I have made a difference, and I will always be a member of COYOTE. The more people come out about an issue, the more power they will have. Sometimes, though, I do get tired of talking about prostitution because it was in my past.

If you're going to get prostitution decriminalized or legalized, there has to be a large body of people behind it. I think one day we will have prostitution decriminalized, if not legalized. Actually, I don't think it will ever really be legalized in the United States because we're so moralistic. Ministers were some of my biggest clients, yet they were preaching to get prostitutes off the streets. I wish that prostitution would become decriminalized or legalized so that I could openly share basic information, or even mentor young women, so they wouldn't have to go through what I went through. At times I have met with people, giving them information, while knowing that I was committing a crime because it's illegal to advise someone on doing illegal activities.

SIOBAHN: In Evelyn C. White's book, *The Black Woman's Health Book*, you mentioned that black prostitutes could be viewed as educators in the black community. What do you think the black community's overall view is of prostitution?

GLORIA: The black community is very downing, very opinionated. However, I think that it's easier to accept a black prostitute than it is to accept a lesbian or gay person in the black community. I think that's because prostitution is about money, and people understand that the reason you're doing it relates to money. But still it's very difficult.

SIOBAHN: How did your family react to you being a prostitute?

GLORIA: I've been very fortunate because my family has always been very supportive. I was on the Donahue show six or seven years ago, and I assumed my grandmother in Waco, Texas, wasn't going to see the show. [laughs] I called my grandmother a couple of weeks after I had been on the show, and she said, "Oh, I saw you on television." I asked what did she think, and she said that she's never been so proud of me. In our family we don't throw away our children for what they have done.

My mother never said the word prostitution, but she knew what I was doing. She was very accepting, and she used to keep all of our kids: six little white kids and three little black kids. She also loved my man; he would bring her roses and food. My father loved him, too. That's another reason I speak out, because my family has been very supportive.

SIOBAHN: You've been published in a few anthologies. I was wondering if you considered yourself a writer.

GLORIA: No, I don't. I think one day I could be a writer; I'm getting more into it than I've ever been, but I don't consider myself to be one now. I do think I have an interesting story to tell, and the older I get the more I want to document it. For years I have been afraid to tell my story because I know that the media just takes the truth and bends it. I don't want people to glorify and exploit my experience. Prostitution to me was a way of making a living, I was solely in it for the money. All the other stuff about power came along with it after a while, not in the beginning. I and most African Americans who get into prostitution are in it because of the money. If we had another way that would make us $50,000 and $60,000 a year, then that's what we would be doing. Prostitution is very difficult; it's a job. I didn't let it destroy me and I wasn't addicted to drugs. I wasn't this horrible little victim who was misused by this pimp. I knew what I was doing. I was grown when I got into it, and grown when I got out.

SIOBAHN: What is your opinion of a lot of the literature coming out about sex workers?

GLORIA: I've been absent lately from COYOTE, so I haven't read a lot of the current things on sex workers. But for the most part what people write is bull. Writers often exploit you and twist your story around: Either the prostitution is all glorified or it's horrible. There's never a happy medium.

SIOBAHN: The reason I asked is because I have a real problem with a lot of the "feminist" literature coming out about the sex industry. The literature coming out now is basically about sexual expression. It's from a middle-class white perspective, which sends the message that all prostitutes are college students who were tired of being a part of the patriarchal capitalist system. They basically wanted a job to allow them to continue their art, write poetry, and write books. I think some of the writing is interesting, but since we live in a white-supremacist society, publishers will take that one experience into account.

GLORIA: I've heard some of my white friends say that they're in prostitution because of the power. Well, for black women it's for the money. We are powerful people, we don't need to get power by standing on no corner. [laughs] The writings are very white, and people need to know that.

SIOBAHN: Can you talk about how you got your position at CAL-PEP?

GLORIA: CAL-PEP came out of COYOTE. There was a conference at Margo St. James's house in 1982. At that time we realized that as soon as people stopped scapegoating white gay men for transmitting AIDS, the next group would be prostitutes—and in fact it was. We started doing support groups, and Margo St. James, Priscilla Alexander, and I wrote a grant to the state, and the state funded us. Our first grant was $30,000 to work with female sex workers, to talk to them about AIDS, and to make them aware that people were scapegoating them for the spread of AIDS. At about this same time, people were interviewing these women and paying them $15–$20 for an interview, but they were using the information wrongly. We wanted to make sure those women were educated as to what was happening.

After the conference at Margo St. James's house, I got a job as an interviewer for a group called Project Aware, which was a research project. One night I was out talking to some of the prostitutes on the stroll, and this one black girl came up to me and said, "I'm positive. That's good, right?" I'm sure people told her what it meant to be HIV positive, but she didn't hear them. She could not communicate or relate to these white people coming down talking to her about AIDS. She didn't know what AIDS was. She couldn't relate to what it meant to be positive or negative. We then felt that it was really important that we do an HIV prevention and education project. CAL-PEP started off doing education and HIV prevention and testing. Now we are also doing research, and we work with people on the street in the Bay Area.

There's about twenty-four of us, and I'm proud to say that some people have been here as long as ten years. We hire ex-prostitutes, ex–IV drug users. We hire people other people wouldn't hire or feel they can't hire. We do outreach in the real sense; we go to where the people are: the street, crack houses. We feel the people on the street are us, so we look like, act like, and walk like the people we serve. We don't discriminate on the basis of gender. We reach out to everybody: transgendered, drug users, prostitutes, lesbians, and gays.

We also do support groups and offer support groups for HIV-positive African American people and their families. We have made a video—called Blood Sisters: Breaking the Silence—about HIV-AIDS, which features eight African American women who touch on every aspect of living with the AIDS virus.

It's easier for us to work with hard-to-reach people. We do not think prostitutes are the carriers of AIDS. In fact, I have not known one woman who was HIV positive only because of prostitution. Other factors, like drug use or being a partner of someone who's HIV positive, always play a part in their HIV status. Prostitutes have been tested in brothels in Nevada since 1988. They are tested every three months, and they have not found one woman who was positive. It's a myth that prostitutes spread AIDS. Prostitutes are actually the people who have been using condoms for years.

SIOBHAN: What do you think makes it hard for prostitutes of color to seek information about AIDS?

GLORIA: I think there is a lot of denial among the African American community and other communities of color when it comes to AIDS. We don't think it is our problem. I'm real concerned about women and men in heterosexual relationships getting it [HIV] from each other. I'm concerned because many people have multiple sex partners. People think that because in the '70s they had multiple sex partners, they can still do that. I'm scared that a lot of people who think they're okay will come down with AIDS. Many [black] people still think AIDS is a white gay male problem, that we're being brainwashed by the white man, and that it's a form of genocide. Many prostitutes feel that they should use condoms with tricks, but not with their intimate partners. Women can be just as bad as men can when it comes to not using condoms. I'm much more concerned with women getting HIV from their intimate partners than from their clients. My fear is also with women on crack who are in denial that they are prostitutes because they're in it for the drugs, not the money. Sometimes they turn tricks without condoms because they don't consider the man to be a trick. We do a lot of education with crack users, and give them condoms to use.

SIOBHAN: Do you feel like a sex workers' movement is happening, and what are your thoughts about the feminist movement of the '70s?

GLORIA: I've always felt that I was a feminist, but what a feminist is to me is not what a feminist is to some people. I love being a woman and I think it's my right to do whatever I want with my body and mind. Many people think that if you're a prostitute you couldn't be a feminist because you're letting people use you. I always felt that I was certainly using them [the customers] as much as they were using me. So who's using whom? That's the art of the game. It has always irritated me when people asked me, "How could you be a feminist and do this?" How could I not be? Women are breadwinners for the most part, and very strong and powerful. Women basically call the shots, and sometimes we let men think that they're calling them.

Hopefully, women in the sex industry will come together more; I see this with the white women, I'm hoping that the black women and women of color will start coming together, as well.

boys stink
Blake Nemec

Mmmmm, I'm very excited to have a wad of cash in my pocket and a hot boy next to me. My pants fit *right*, and I *know* how to work what's inside of them.

He looks cute as usual with a red-and-white checkered pair of loafer Vans, stretchy black Levis that snug loose his hot flat Jewish ass, and a tight T-shirt that grabs his big manhandleable lower back fat. He's my boy and I'm holding his thigh.

"You smell weird," he says.

"What?"

"You smell like shower-box soap."

"That's weird, I dunno." I say, but I'm jumping out of my skin now—feeling disgusting and a shower box–soap drool.

"Cleo bought this weird soap," I say. "Do you hate it?"

"No, I don't care." But he takes a sip of beverage when he says it, how he says a lie.

Fuck, I shouldn't have come over right after my trick at the hot tubs. Fuck fuck, I want to leave. I go to the bathroom and wash with his soap. I go and sit back down. I'm sweating. A sweaty linoleum boy.

Oh god, I'm freaking out, but not leaving. We're watching, I should say he's watching *elimiDATE* and I'm watching the bubbles advertising the dumb date's actions. It's too much—he's laughing.

"I'm gonna go."

"What's going on?"

"Nothing. I mean, I don't want to stay if I smell like shit."

"Blake. I don't care, come here with your bad smelling soap skin." And he pulls me toward him. I'm in hell.

"No, I gotta go." Pause. I stand up. Stare. Turn around. Just standing there looking at him, then looking at all his toys all shiny and colorful, looking at me without cum or awful smelling soap stuck to them. Shiny plastic faggot cowboys, horses, and the vacuuming tranny girl that I gave him. And then back to him, who must now know that I turned a trick, I mean he knows my trick clothes but trick

161

clothes become your street clothes because you get paid good cash money in them and then you're like, hey, these are *my* clothes. Not my *trick* clothes, I mean, I wore them for a trick because they are *hot* so here I am. Hot. Right?

"Yeah, I gotta go."

We're at his door now.

"Don't worry, I'm just feeling introspective, I have to go." I say.

He slumps, and shakes his head slowly and around with wide open eyes, his I don't know what's going on, but I'm smart enough to not say anything look. Great, he doesn't know what's going on yet. *Leave, leave fast,* before you break down and tell the truth and are still there in your hot-tub scent with the psychic toys staring at you.

"Okay," I sigh, and shrug my shoulders like *shit*, just when I thought I wanted to be next to someone here I am feeling the need to be alone.

"Bye. Don't worry about me."

"Okay Blake, okay." He really really sweetly says with more wide-eyed wonder. Which is sick, and I want to stay and fuck him. I look back at him with my mouth open.

"Yeah, okay, bye," I say quickly. Mousy. And grab the door getting stuck with my bike and feel my angst rushing out with me—a mob of shameful hooker energy like a suction and then the door closes but I don't remember pulling it closed.

meeting rita
Eileen Myles

I didn't want to think about this. Now she was making me nervous. She said the nice guy from the hotel bar went home to California or someplace after his work was done, but he did something funny. He gave me four hundred and fifty dollars. You're kidding, I gasped. For what. That was exactly my question, she whooped. She really did whoop, and she knocked over her drink then. Maybe we should go. Yeah, I nodded. A skinny really hip-looking girl in a dancer top put the check down in a brown plastic tray. We were a couple of losers. My pleasure the girl said, when Rita plopped a couple more twenties down.

Are you hungry. Her name was Rita. When she said my name is Rita she drooped her long hand towards me like she'd been in business thirty years. We were walking down 8th Street now.

He told me I might need it, she said. Meaning the money, I asked. And I did need it, she said. Of course, I shrugged. So I got my own room in the Carlyle that night and next day I returned to the bar. Another guy sat down. Blond with a crewcut, she explained. He was just a guy from New Jersey, but he preferred to spend his work nights in the city. I told him I just arrived, he said let me show you around. He brought me to the local. Locale, I corrected. She just looked in my eyes, she had very pale blue eyes, and all they said was you are so completely missing the point. I'm sure I was.

She didn't care about the poetry field at all. The second guy wanted to fuck all night. That's cool, she interjected, but in the morning he said, you're a hooker, right.

I just lost my bag, she explained to me like I was him. And what are you going to do about that, he said and he shoves two fifty in my hand. I put it in my purse, she shrugged.

The bartender who was a very nice man told me that if I stayed around much longer that I would probably get in trouble. I told the people at the front desk you're my niece. He smiled putting another drink in front of her. And they don't believe me.

I checked into the Warwick she said. It's not as nice. The Carlyle was *old-style*. By now I'm thinking she's as bad as me. But, a man staying there, a very nice man she nods to me, has a business associate who is coming into town tomorrow—an Italian, well actually two Italians. Italian handbag salesmen. And I have a date with both of them, but I have to bring a friend. She smiled so sweetly at me, just with her lips. Just a little tug of sweetness occurred, almost a hum. She was a little crazy, but god she was good. I think she wants me to be a whore.

It's just a date she said. I don't know anyone. We don't have to do anything—these guys, they're just lonely. We can have dinner, you can see for yourself. Go to a discotheque. But I don't want to meet them alone. Now she looked a little scared and desperate. She was working me. When your brother—

My stepbrother.

When your stepbrother, forgive me, told me he had a sister who lived downtown who's a poet—

You just figured I was broke.

Well, yeah.

In the massage parlor the woman doing reception was a blonde who I assumed to be Swedish and she kind of looked like Faye Dunaway. I had already put on a bathing suit and I was wearing some kind of heels with straps across

165

the toes. I felt white and gross, but still you know how you know you are young. Guys would come in and sit down in their suits. Pairs of guys. Twice they pointed at me to the woman at the desk. Can we have her? How do you look at a person who says that. It's like you don't get embarrassed. You're kind of hiding in yourself. That's exactly what I was doing. No, she's getting trained. I am? They were lead into other rooms off the side of the lobby, then she said come on. She took my hand. She had this black dress on, and her blonde hair was swept back and she looked like a lady. We got into this little room. Eileen this is Don. He was lying on the bed, really like a surgical table. Hi Eileen he said, grasping for my fingers. She pitched her head to the right. Why don't you go in there and get comfortable. I looked down. I was standing in my maroon bathing suit. It was basically a dancer thing. It was called a maillot. Lots of people had lofts then in New York, and those people were two kinds, painters and dancers. It was like girls were walking around looking like dancers, and they took classes and that's what they were waitressing for. I understood this idea and I dressed like these girls for a while. I just think fashion is invisibility. If you want to go over there, or stay here, you just slip on the uniform and slip off into the crowd.

Rita said we were getting drinks. There's a place called Fridays she said in another hotel. They have a disco. In a hotel? My feet felt like lead, but I was being a girl so I kept kicking them forward, smiling.

In the massage parlor I was standing alone in a tiny room with my towel around me. I can't go out. What am I going to do, walk out and go hi. I always hear about men feeling humiliated by the army, or something. They should try being female. I went in holding my towel. She goes, okay dear, but her eyes were flashing like she was scared. I was taking too long. Don was on the bed and she opened his towel. His eyes gleamed too, but I bet he was excited. Eileen's new Don, so we're showing her the ropes. She gave him a little peck on the cheek like he was an old friend. Hope you don't mind. Hi Eileen he said again, to say he approved.

He had this little sprout of a dick. I think most of them are small. She put her strong white hand around it and then said Eileen, put your hand on top of mine. We were jerking him off together. Ahh he groaned that's good, I guess pretending he was getting a massage. Soon the woman and I were in a rhythm. I was her little nurse standing to her left. We were hip to hip, pumping away. Oh yes, yes, he went. Then she went down on him. Oh no, I thought. It was like the contents of my brain turned inside out. I can't give blow jobs for a living. I can't do this. I've got to go, I said.

Hold on, Don, she said. Is something wrong. She had me pinned between the little door to the other room and this room. I'm okay, I just have to go, I can't do this. She said oh Baby, and put her arms around me. I'm standing there in a towel. Do you like girls, she said, holding me close. I did.

Attilio kept looking back, smiling. We were walking up some side street in the fifties from one hotel bar to another. Eventually he grabbed my hand and the two of us walked along. All of this was conducted in little English. He'd push his hand in his jacket and pull out his pack. Cigarette? I had the cigarette jammed in my mouth crooked and he had some fuel lighter that smelled. He kept going *plunk, plunk* and even opened his suit jacket and I jammed my head in to get it lit. For what? It was a very unsatisfying cigarette.

Rita reveled in her capacity to look normal. She was laughing gaily with Freddy. She might've been wearing his suit jacket by now and they were swinging their hands together, just a pair on a date. A traveling handbag salesman and a whore. They looked great. I remember as a kid looking in the window of a travel agency. There was a poster of a woman standing on a beach with flowers around her neck. It looked like Hawaii. I was never sure if it was the woman they were selling the vacation to, the woman who had succeeded, or if she was the woman you got if you bought this ticket. I was like a ticket Attilio found on the street on a trip to New York. Would I dust his ticket off. Good as new, I gleamed like a bellboy. Only a person who thinks like me can sell her own her ass thinking she's a cultural critic. Or even weirder feeling she's a man. I would be a man if I wrote. And being a man would render these steps I'm taking towards a place called Tuesday's—Tuesday's in my masculine hands would be literature. Each little step was a coin. Ting, the door flung open. It was art.

We went to the hotel. By now I'd succumbed to only walking hand in hand. We had moved around each other all evening: Attilio and I. His green jacket shone and flickered. Constantly I looked at his shoes, pointed and I have to admit, a little scuffed. I stood with him and Rita and Frank in front of a row of brown elevators as if it were a rocket launch. Everybody here knows what's going on except me. I mean I could say no to the story right now or I can obediently go along with it and when the door opens, walk on. It was an unbearable wait, with a substantial amount of human traffic in the yellow lobby. Rita was probably waiting to see if I would bolt. At this moment we were standing in a battle of nerves. She had probably already set her terms. I was the only outsider on this tour. I could say I think I need to go home. Sorry thank you for the lovely evening, all the drinks and the powdered scrambled eggs I guess it was a bagel the fakest bagel I ever had in my life. The four elevators a rusty reddish brown hung there like stone. I guess I'm just going to get on. No one seems to be saying anything. I guess they all think I'm just going to go up. I'm just turning into a whore right at this moment. I'm just turning into a whore. Foom, the doors open and we got on. We rode up in silence and Rita smiled. I can't believe my step-brother got me into this shit. Will I ever tell him. He will never know. The elevator stopped on the 16th floor. We're getting off here. See you guys, Rita leaned in and pecked me a kiss cause we were friends. Foop. The doors closed. Attilio leaned back against the elevator. Oh my god, he's ignoring me. He looked at me out of the corner of his eyes. It is okay he asked kindly. I really think he did. I said yes.

Are all hotel rooms grey. Or maybe it's mauve. It's a pale little color. And something is gold, maybe the drapes. And tall thunderous lampshades on, the light, to remember this is home. Big public globes of peace. You'd like another drink. He leaned back on the bed. By now he had thrown his jacket on the chair. Loosened his tie. I said yes. He lifted a bottle of vermouth from the night table. You like he asked. Sure I said, just like an American. He poured it in my glass and put his hand on my head and soon the light went out.

he first time I ever kissed was outside in a park in my town and it was in the fall and the kid was about a year younger than me and kind of cute but he had pimples and I generally felt that his family was poor. He came from a whole family of brothers and many of the girls who were in my gang, mostly sisters and then Franny the girl next door, they all were, all these girls went steady with all these boys and that meant simply that you kissed and some small bit of metal, a tie clip, a ring was exchanged. And all of this was alien to me but I was part of this group and wanted what had happened to them to happen to me so when it was pointed out that I could have Wayne I took him so I could have the experiences I seemed to need to be a girl in my gang. I mention all of this to describe the kiss, my first. My first I could own as mine. He meant to kiss me, and would do it again. But why. Probably also because he could. Our little lips met to no purchase. I mean no revulsion, or storm, or revelation. Just warm dry adolescent skin in the cold fall, just before supper. A couple of duck bills, smack. He shoved something at me, which did make me ill, perhaps a tie clip, but it meant that the deal was sealed. And I got out of it as quickly as I could; going steady was something I had done. With Wayne. Oh yeah.

Attilio was kissing any girl on the bed and it seemed that this would pass. The unevent of sex with an adult stranger, putting his soft drunken tongue in my mouth. Somehow we got our clothes off and actually think got under the covers. In retrospect it was like married sex. The ribbony silk that trimmed the blanket and the hard dryness of the clean hotel sheets were my friends. His hands moved aimlessly along my body, touching my ordinary female chest. My breasts weren't large, but I never had wished they were. I had no sympathy for his possible disappointment. I was the body he'd been paying for all night. It wasn't like he bought me. He rented me. Each drink was the accomplishment of another forty minutes or an hour in which I agreed to stay with him who was perhaps eleven years older than me and probably married. I think I asked him if he was and he said he was married. I asked him if he had any kids and he said yes. I think he went down on me. I sort of remember it. My legs being boringly open on that bed. It really was a different experience of being a body. That I had maybe overtly agreed with Rita to do all this and silently conspired with Attilio, but mostly it reminded me of Wayne and years later of a performing; making out in a movie: the smells of a woman I didn't want. Not one I *didn't want* either. But like Wayne we were inscribed together on a piece of graph paper like ducks drawn on a table cloth for later embroidering which I guess is now.

In the dark, the dark of that bed I think of grey, more colorless than childhood, we actually did it. I think of his penis which I believe was small but I thought of as Italian, kind of shapely and uncircumcised, is that possible? I've seen hundreds of penises yet I still don't think I can tell the difference, but that makes me more of a lesbian than a whore, or someone congenitally disinterested in stepping up to the mike. He pushed his not so hard part into my not so defined part. I thought of this sexual experience occurring in folds. It was like sex between two flowers. Not beautiful, but not unfriendly, occurring in slow weighty cascading silk. Which was our lethargic drunken inevitable sex. We grunted and plunged I think, not for long, I think I allowed and even enjoyed it in that I was a witness to my body taking part in an animal unknown having made a deal as if I were my father and I had sold my daughter in exchange for some furs and a bottle of wine. I wasn't so much in season as drifting through the yard, and the thought grew bright in my father's head, why not her. I am that one.

I was in bed alone. You know how you can kick your legs to the left and the right in a huge hotel bed, but still you feel a little lost. I looked at the clock, 5:30. It was summer so it was already light. Now there was blue a huge square of pale morning blue and Attilio Viola was sitting on a chair in front of it having a cigarette. There was a balcony and he had the door shoved open and his smoke was blowing out. He didn't know if I was watching him and he didn't care. His leg was folded over his knee. You could tell he just enjoyed being a man in a body. Probably went to the beach.

With his family. Maybe he had a girlfriend in Italy. Sort of a cream-coloured guy. He was just sitting there smoking in his cotton briefs and a sleeveless T-shirt. A thin gold chain around his neck with a tiny gold medal. Not quite getting old, but he will. Soft rounded shoulders. He's looking out at New York. What a great city with its plunging skyline and secret roofs and signs and cars already on their way. I suspected it was a melancholy moment for him. We had all drunk a lot. He probably does this all the time, picks up girls in strange cities and pays for them. He said he's going to London next. I looked at him and I thought about that, the paying, and I couldn't imagine how I would bring it around. Hey can you give me—I don't know, three hundred bucks would feel right. Rent and some stuff. What am I worth.

But he just looked sad looking out over this city that wasn't his. He was northern Italian. It was so far away. He looked back at me for a moment and gave me a little pirate grin. Hey he said in his quick Italian and then he returned to his smoke. I began to get dressed. I didn't ask for it. I said, hey. And got dressed. I left him in the window just like that. I left him alone with his view.

the night that plays like ping-pong in my head
Mattilda, a.k.a. Matt Bernstein Sycamore

I wake up and I've wet my bed, one of my socks is filled with piss, the bathroom floor is soaked. I almost pass out on the bus, come home and sleep for twenty hours. All because of this trick who brought tequila. And I don't even drink tequila. He came over and started chopping limes. I said I'm only gonna have a shot or two, put down that knife. He said I'd never hurt you—you know that, don't you? I said I'm just afraid of knives. He said you can tell by the eyes, look me in the eyes. His eyes were practically glazed over. He poured me a shot, handed me a lime

175

and asked if I had any sea salt. Before I knew it, the bottle was close to empty, I was on the ceiling licking salt off my hand and chewing limes. He tried to stick a hundred dollar bill up my ass, and I went to the bathroom. Came back and the money was gone. I said did you just put that hundred back in your pocket? He said what hundred? At some point he gave back the money, like it hadn't been in my asshole or anything. Then he said I'll give you another hundred if you get hard again. I'd just come in his mouth, and I hate having my dick touched after I come, but for an extra hundred, whatever. I said pour me another shot, and then he was sucking my dick again, before I knew it I was hard. He wanted me to fuck him. I tried, but couldn't stay hard: no big shock. We took a break, he asked me if I'd go to Mexico with him. We'd sit on the beach and drink margaritas all day. I said first you'll have to give me that other hundred. He said you're not charging me by the hour. I said I just got hard. He said yeah, but you didn't fuck me. I looked him in the eyes. He looked away. That's when I got dramatic. I said look me in the eyes, and I stared right at him, right at his eyes. He couldn't hold my gaze. I said the eyes don't lie, and I kept staring right at him. He got all nervous, kept repeating that I hadn't fucked him, he'd already given me a hundred. I was through. I said listen bitch, you better take out that hundred or I'm not calling you again. He said I don't have another hundred. I said do you think you can work me? I said honey I've been turning tricks since I was fourteen, and I went into the kitchen for effect. Or water. Then I came back, picked up that tequila and took one big swig. I said you and I both know, and I looked him right in the eyes, you and I both know that it's not about the money. He reached for the bottle and I pulled it away. I was swinging the bottle in the air, if he'd taken out the money right then, I would have ripped it to shreds.

degrade Emi Koyama

degradation
is not trading sex for money

but it is exchange

of social security number for food

degradation

is not stripping away minidress

but it is not having curtain

covering me in a public shower

degradation

is not faking orgasms on the phone

but it is faking compliance

with the court order

degradation

is not even being raped on the street

but it is the doctor asking me

"why does it bother you if you fuck

strangers anyway?"

jimmy Nomy Lamm

d^{ear jimmy,}

where are you? i've been back on with the service for a week and a half and you haven't called yet. i know i was gone for a while but i guess i just thought you would always be there. i know it was complicated, but you have to admit there was a genuine feeling in there. i wonder how you are. i feel like i'm betraying your confidence, telling all these people about you. but we never promised each other anything.

Sometimes I think about him, walking around in the world in his business suit. I wonder if I would recognize him if I saw him. Would I be able to tell? Other people might guess that there is something churning hard under the surface. They would probably never guess what it was, mostly because they wouldn't want to know. But I know. And there is still a part of me that thinks that it matters. All the nights he would call me from the middle of his escapades so I could encourage, prompt, humiliate, degrade, pass the phone around to my friends so they could laugh at him. Make him cum.

Why would he need me, if he has his mistresses, his roommate, his dogs, his snake, his conferences, his cucumbers? But I'm getting ahead of myself.

Let me introduce him.

The phone rings. I answer it and hear a mechanical chime. Press one. The dispatcher comes on, "I have a request for you, it's James Roberts, he can go as long as he wants." The phone chimes again and we are connected.

"Hey Jimmy," I say. "How's it going?"

"Mmmm," he says. "oh, oh, oh."

"What are you doing?"

"Playing," he says. I hear it. Unevenness of voice and breath. Something being done to him.

"That sounds fun," I say in my girly voice. "Tell me about it."

Imagine, now, that you are me. You live on the ground floor in a neighborhood where Cubs fans and frat guys parade around, frequenting the Irish pubs, the Mardi Gras-themed sports bar next door, and occasionally the palm reader upstairs. You live alone and barely pay rent on your freezing-cold roach-hole apartment by working five nights a week taking calls. You are in a relationship with a female-bodied genderqueer who you call your boyfriend. You have phone sex with men in the pantry while your lover watches TV and listens to your fake orgasms. The work suits you especially in the winter because the cold makes your back hurt and it's better not to have to leave the house.

"Ohhhh," Jimmy gurgles. "I'm getting fucked." He sucks in air through his teeth and whimpers. I can't remember the last time I had actual sex with my lover. My disability has been particularly disabling lately, and the phone sex has driven a bit of a wedge.

"You're pathetic," I tell him.

"I'm sorry mommy. I know, I'm a pathetic faggot," Jimmy's voice is little.

"That's right, you're a dirty, pathetic faggot," I parrot. He enjoys this technique—repeating key phrases back and forth. I listen to him grunt as he gets pounded and I get a clear picture. I know what he's doing.

"Boris is about to cum, mommy," he tells me.

"I knew it, you fucking pervert," I say. Boris is Mistress Tabitha's dog. A Great Dane.

The next line is unwritten. There is no summing up, no justification, no one true feeling about the experience of listening to a man get fucked by a dog. Understand me. When you are on a phone-sex call you are experiencing it, you are complicit. You can laugh about it later, but during the call it's a reality. If you were me, by now you would have listened, dozens of times, to this man stroke, suck, and get fucked by this Great Dane. You would have encouraged him, degraded him, rode through it with him. The first time I experienced this, I felt like something in me was fundamentally changed. I didn't stop it. I couldn't. I didn't want to.

A memory came back to me, of a dream I had when I was thirteen. A dog with a boner. It built up and built up until he came with a bright shower of color, leaving me with the feeling of shame and release. My friend and I would always tell our dreams to each other on the walk to school. That day I was embarrassed. I hemmed and hawed and when I finally told her she looked at me like I was gross and said, "That's it"?

The dog cums. That's it. Shoots a load of jizz up Jimmy's

ass. I listen to Jimmy groan and take it, then slide off to suck the cum off the dog's cock as it softens.

"Oh, mommy it's so good. It tastes so good. It's sweeter and more liquidy than a man's cum." No. Don't want to know. Shut off. It's just words. Blah blah blah. La la la. Jimmy gives Boris a Milk-Bone and says "good boy," then decides to climb onto the giant dildo he has suctioned to his yoga ball. I think this is a great idea and go "boing, boing" with him as he rides his bouncy ball, telling me stories about a conference he went to recently with Mistress Tabitha where they did a demonstration with Boris. He is particularly proud because he won the Biggest Slut trophy for getting fucked by every man (and dog) there.

If you are a phone-sex operator reading this you may be thinking to yourself, This is all in this guy's head. And that's what I thought at first. But over time I came to see the difference between the men with hyperactively surreal fantasy lives and Jimmy, who I believe actually did at least 90 percent of what he talked about. Rather than grasping for stereotypes and glamorizations, as many men do, I feel Jimmy was reaching for every real experience that he could possibly pull into his fantasy. He wants everyone, everything involved in his sex life.

"Oh, mommy, is Stacy there?" Jimmy begs. Stacy is the name I gave to my lover after the time I told Jimmy my boy-friend was there. But when he heard the voice in the background he said, "That sounds like a girl." Ever since he has begged to talk to Stacy.

"Yeah, she's here," I say. "Stacy, Jimmy wants to talk to you."

"Tell him I think he's a dirty faggot," my boyfriend calls and Jimmy groans.

He insists on talking to her and I ask how much it's worth to him. He promises me a thirty-dollar tip and I get "Stacy" on the phone long enough to spit a couple of awkward half-hearted insults at him. The phone is handed back to me and Jimmy is ecstatic.

"Oh mommy that was so hot," I can tell he's getting closer. "Oh mommy, talk in that baby voice, please, mommy," I can hear the ball squeaking in the background.

"Dat's a good widdo baybee," I say.

"Oh, I love you mommy," he coos.

"Good widdo baybee, good boy," I say.

"I love you mommy."

"I love you baby."

"I love you mommy."

"I love you baby."

A friend once asked me "Is that okay for you?" when I said that I sometimes tell clients I love them. It's not hard for me. I don't even feel like I'm lying. Doesn't mean I have any intention of taking the relationship further.

But I guess you could say that Jimmy and I took it further. It just happened naturally. One night, while he recounted the exploits of his weekend, I said, "You use condoms, right?" His voice changed then, and he said he did, usually, probably not as much as he should. "It's important, Jimmy. You need to be safe." I didn't know how this would go over. I don't usually interject wake-up calls into phone-sex sessions. But after that night he would often refer to it, telling me, "and I made them use condoms, and I thought about you, and it made me feel so good that you cared."

Not everything about him was quite so sweet and tender. My boundaries were pushed, often, like the period when he was always shoving a snake up his ass. A real live snake with slithery skin and a flicking forked tongue. I said, "Isn't that suffocating the snake?" and he said, "No, they go in holes naturally, they burrow." I went along with it and listened to him take fifteen inches, groaning as it wriggled into him. I drew the line at him fucking the dog. I said, "It's one thing to let it fuck you, but a dog can't consent to you fucking it." He seemed to get the point, though he argued a little, but ultimately he didn't do it, at least not on the phone with me. He was as desperate for my approval as he was for my disdain, so he would apologize profusely every time he knew he crossed a line.

So after a year and a half of talking to him a few times

a week, as weird and deep and twisted and real as the connection was, he just felt like a normal part of my life. Not taking up any more energy than he was paying for, and giving me good stories for later. My relationship with my lover ended and I got into another one with a trans man who would sometimes get on the phone and be Jimmy's daddy. Jimmy paid $50 for that. I'd go on tour and come back and Jimmy would always call within a couple of days, saying, "I missed you mommy." Sometimes he would disappear for a few weeks and then reemerge with more crazy stories and new fetishes being explored. One time he told me he had taken to shoving a cucumber up his ass and going to the mall with it inside him. "I saw two people I knew," he told me, groaning with the memory, "and I talked to them. It was so hot." I wondered what those people thought of the interaction.

He was insatiable. There was no endpoint, he was in constant expansion. He attended frequent sex gatherings where he was always the star, dressed up in his wigs, heels and hose, thigh-high boots and lipstick. He even managed to get action as a regular suit-wearing dude staying at hotels on business trips; I loved his story about the knock-knock game that preceded a porn-watching and blow-job fest with the businessman in the room next to his. One particularly tender moment happened on Christmas night, when I got to inaugurate his new Real Doll, by naming it Trent and making him say "I love you Trent" while he fucked its tight rubber hole. I marveled at the breadth of his vision and the depth of his appetite. I loved him for living it, for doing what felt good, as much as I was taken aback by the scope of his entitlement, access, and compartmentalization. I bet he's a very good businessman.

At a certain point that winter, I started to get really burnt-out on phone sex. I was sad that my relationship wasn't working and that I had more intimacy with random dudes than I did with my long-distance lover. I was grossed out to have their issues occupying space in my precious new studio apartment. And I was pissed off that I had to struggle so fucking hard to claim my sexuality, when these men have the resources to occupy other people's space with their unexamined shit. I couldn't help feeling invaded with every call, and my cute, sweet, friendly persona became more bitter and monotone.

Nights passed without intrigue while Jimmy found new outlets. A kinky new couple who he played with. They met over the Internet, then at a local café and went back to their place together, where he fucked the husband and the wife fucked him. "Uhhh, mommy, it was so hot," he gurgles at me. I stare blankly at the computer screen, click click click, playing solitaire. "Wow."

"Oh and mommy, I told them about Boris, and she wants to try it, wouldn't that be hot mommy?"

"Mm-hmm." Click click.

"Wouldn't that be hot, to watch Boris fuck her pussy?" I can hear his hand slapping his cock. Another childhood memory comes back to me. I'm ten years old at my dad's softball practice in the park. I'm petting this big white fluffy dog who knocks me over and keeps jumping up on top of me. It's freaking me out, and my dad and all his friends are laughing so hard it takes them forever to pull him off of me. "What was he doing?" I ask. "He was trying to hump you." I hide my face from all the laughing men. Any one of them could be Jimmy.

"You make me sick," I tell him.

"I'm sorry mommy," he says, groaning as he cums.

And then I didn't hear from him for a while. I'd sign on every night expecting his call, but nothing. Just a bunch of giantess fetishists and CBT enthusiasts, pedophiles and cross-dressers. Weeks went by. I was glad that Jimmy wasn't calling. I didn't have the energy to act like I cared what he was doing or make him feel loved.

I have to pause and ask you Jimmy. how are you, now? do you feel loved? is it forgotten? are you fixated? haunted? healed? you know that this is the part of the story that ties the knot. a part of me is true to you always.

'm in the middle of making dinner the next time Jimmy calls. "What are you doing mommy?" he asks, hearing the chop chop of the knife. I start talking about how I'm cutting vegetables so I can boil him in a pot of soup like Bugs Bunny. He doesn't totally go for it but he's not put off. "I missed you mommy."

"I missed you too," I say, deadpan. Then, to be nice, "Where have you been?"

"Something bad happened, and I had to take a break."

I stop my chopping. "I'm sorry," I tell him, seriously, leaving open space in case he wants to say more.

"You remember that couple I was playing with?" I say yes. "Well I went over one day, and they tied me up, and a bunch of their friends came over, and it wasn't play. . . . It was like they were mad at me."

They kept him tied up for ten hours. He was repeatedly raped and beaten by the couple and five of their friends. When they finally let him leave he was bruised and bleeding and almost unconscious. He hadn't told his roommate or mistress about the couple, so nobody knew where he was. Oh Jimmy. Poor baby. I hope he can hear the genuine compassion in my voice when I tell him how horrible that sounds.

I have no training in dealing with this. One time a

nineteen-year-old with a developmental disability called me and basically reported a trauma that was happening to him in his home. He hung up the second I said it was wrong for his parents to do that to him. I agonized over that choice afterwards—was it just his fantasy? Was I shaming him?—it seemed so real.

In this case I can tell this is not Jimmy's fantasy. He's confiding in me, as someone he trusts. I wonder what it will be like to go back to phone sex with him again after this conversation. He says his mistresses have been really nice to him while he recovered, and he just went to his first sex party again a couple nights ago.

"There was a head mistress, the lady who owned the house, and I got locked in a cage with her eighteen-year-old daughter," he says, with that telltale gurgle. I brace myself. I don't like this eighteen-year-old-daughter-in-a-cage situation. La la la. "We could barely move, the cage was so small, we could just wiggle around, and they made me fuck her," slap slap slap.

"Oh, that sounds hot," I'm not totally lying. Despite or maybe because of the creep-out factor, it is a hot story.

"It was so hot," he growls. "I fucked the shit out of her."

"Yeah?"

"I fucked her and fucked her, I fucked her raw, I made her scream . . . "

I go along with his story. His voice sounds different, there's another layer to it that wasn't there before. Then it softens. He wants to be humiliated. I can't do it with the fervor I used to. I feel sad and tender towards him. I talk about sucking his cock, one of my favorite phone-sex activities, something we never really do together, and he cums and says he'll call me again soon. I think that was the last time we talked.

■

I don't really even expect you to remember me. it's been eight months and you're a busy guy. you've probably had at least a couple new better mommies who only know the now-jimmy, not the then-jimmy. it's okay. i hope you never read this. but somehow, magically, i hope you know it. you have a witness.

love,
mommy katie

golden
Ariel Smith

I am standing

strong, fresh, and golden

in the day glow softness

of the kiddie stroll

tight skin

bathed in the sickly, soothing yellow of streetlights

we're all here

scrubbed shiny

made up like perfect, pretty dollies

I be chapped lips and fishnets

pinkie toes swollen and sore from digging into the edges

of these high heeled boots

$49.95 at the store down on Hastings

god I hate these fucking shoes

don't like feeling all wobbly and unsure when I walk

like some little girlie playing dress up

wanna feel big and swollen inside myself

sexy, dangerous monster

huge powerful strides

glowing self confident

then

familiar sound

car tires cut slick through pools of oily water

slowly, slowing

take your pick

there's so many lined up

pink, powdery candies

waiting to be drawn into the warm danger of your

      moving vehicle

leaving you with traces of our sugary sweetness

I lean over

big, shiny smile wasted on you

my long hair brushing against cold metal of your

      window frame

"how old are you baby?"

"thirteen, fourteen?"

"i'm how ever old you want me to be"

"$60 for the best head of your life"

these words fall from my dry, painted lips and then

laid before you

my words small poems laid before you

on cold, cracked cement

eye contact

drawn in by my prototypical innocence

car door swings open and tonight fear rushes

tonight fear rushes all hot and demanding like

     a fever

biting at my ankles like a bad dream

but I step over it

on it

crush it, crush it

put all the weight in my twelve-year-old body

     on that fear and crush it

slide in beside you your warm hand on my thigh

talking all light and empty like Styrofoam

     crumbling

we pull way and that fear is left dishevelled

     beside my six

with just traces

of pink, sugar sweet, powder.

advice Kirk Read

Okay, I'm just going to be blunt about some basic rules. You should try to avoid doing drugs with clients. On the surface, it seems like a good idea on several levels. Free drugs with nice enough people and the promise of a multiple-hour session because that's how it goes when drugs are involved. How do you resist a $400 payday after three hours with someone who's just given you a free tab of ecstasy, someone who really loves you in that moment and wants to look at you and maybe even cry? But this is the thing, you'll end up fucking them without a condom because if you have any sense you also popped a

Viagra, knowing that they wanted to get fucked and these days, chemistry being what it is, why leave things to chance? I don't care what people say, when it's X and speed, condoms are simply impossible. People don't like to admit that because it's part of the puritan stuff they're trying to escape from. That's why safe-sex billboards don't work for tweakers and fags. They become part of the din of the world that they're trying to escape. More parental voices in the choir. Or, for those of us who are way more rigid and judgmental than both our parents put together, those billboards give us more material, brand new pieces of verbal self-harassment.

I once met this guy in Palm Springs on a very emotionally messy work trip where I saw eight people in six days or something like that. He had this mansion in a gated community and basically he wanted to put toys up my butt while he smoked cigarettes. Which was fine. Then a few years later I saw him again up here in San Francisco and he said he'd switched and was bottoming a lot. He had been seeing an escort that he'd really fallen in love with who'd fucked him for the first time in years, and I was thinking, yeah, you got fucked bareback, that's what that means. This guy got fucked bareback and released himself from a lot of years of shame about how irresponsible he was for having the audacity to enact his jerk-off fantasies, intact, without bleeping, which are what condoms are, a kind of bleep.

He, and I should just give him a name, but I'm a hooker and won't use the real name because a) I'm a total professional, and b) I don't remember it at the moment. I'd have to search my AOL account for it. I'm an electronic packrat. My grandparents had their house condemned in rural Virginia because they had too much old furniture in their backyard. Rats in pianos. For me, it's more about an unruly hard drive. Anyway, I'm going to call this man Paul.

I got to the hotel, the Hyatt I think, yeah, because I remember that there were two towers and that hotel is notorious for architectural confusion. You get a room number like 2641 and it doesn't mean the 26th floor, it means the sixth floor of the second tower. Or is it the Hilton that's so daunting?

Paul wanted to do a tab of ecstasy and I was in one of my liberated moods, justifying it, thinking *I really shouldn't be such a prude, I really need to let go of all my good-boy tendencies and airs*. It's so out of line with my performance of myself, it's so disjointed, this constant pressure to have my teachers write glowing things on the back of my report card. Those things were way more important to my father than my actual grades. Dad wanted to see that the teacher had taken the time to write in blue cursive, "Your son is such a joy to have in class! So willing to help! So kind to his classmates!" Clients have a website where they write those kinds of comments about escorts but I don't even want to get into that right now because I feel like I'm getting ahead of myself.

We take the ecstasy and I secretly take a Viagra in the bathroom because I know that my dick turns into mush on ecstasy. Like a pile of steamed mushrooms on a plate in a Chinese restaurant, useless to a man who's flown all the way up here to get fucked and feel loved because he's getting his prostate battered. His lover doesn't do that anymore. I think one of his lovers died at some point. Isn't that a safe assumption? There's all this other stuff going on with these people. You walk down the street and people are just graveyards, really. I used to smile at everyone and think that being cheerful could make the world a better place and now I see all sorts of spirits swirling around their bodies. Little blue fish swimming laps around their heads, knives sticking out of their cheeks, skin rashes and burns like planes have landed on their bellies. I guess I always sensed this stuff but now I see it. You have to be careful with other people.

This man told me he loved me half an hour into me fucking him. He couldn't believe that I was staying hard. He said that the escort he'd fallen madly in love with couldn't stay hard and so they'd just cuddle and cry and talk about Italy. That's a little much for me at this point with someone I'm only going to see maybe once a year. In the old days I would have been right there with him, leaving bits of my kidneys and liver everywhere—not indiscriminate, but open (really probably too open sometimes).

Guys on ecstasy have a hard time shooting their loads, so you don't have a clear endpoint, the way you do with guys who are just tripping on shame and release. You shoot your load and they start dabbing at you with a white hotel washcloth like you're a wet countertop and if that doesn't make you want to go home then you've got low standards.

I used a condom with him, with Paul. Is that what I called him? Is that what you think his name is? Paul. I knew I was going to fuck him and the risk is so much lower when you're a top, and it feels so much better and if I'm on ecstasy it's going to be a challenge to stay hard anyway and I do feel this warm sense of love for him right now. Back then, all this was going through my head. It's a kind of calculus, figuring out what to do. He was probably getting barebacked by that escort and other guys, too, so even if I wasn't particularly at risk for HIV, there could be other critters up there, things a pill or a shot can't banish, unsightly warts and herpes and things that live on and on beyond the moment. And you add up all the itching, you consider the discomfort, later, of being in situations where people you're with are guessing that you have a wart on the head of your dick but not saying any-thing. You add up all those moments for the rest of your life and you put it all on the digital scale you use to weigh quarter ounces of pot and you write it all down, then ask your-self is it worth it for a better sensation on your dick? 'Cause condoms are really about tops feeling better. The difference in sensation is more of an issue for the top.

And if you're not attached to having someone shoot cum in your ass, you're better off. I mean, there's the whole male pregnancy thing, lots of guys want to please everyone, lots of guys just don't want to jostle the Grand Mystery with a single word. Those guys shouldn't do drugs with their cli-ents. That's the bottom line from Uncle Kirk. If having some-one you just met shoot cum up your ass makes you feel like a better person, if it gives you this glow of being pregnant and taking on the legacy of an entire generation of men, if that cum is more than an ending, if that cum is more than a relief and a grade on the report card, if you feel like you need that handwritten note from the teacher, if you want your dad to rub your head and tell you how proud he is, these are all good reasons not to do drugs with a client.

my first porn film
Jennifer Blowdryer

For a hot, dead-broke nineteen-year-old girl, it's cheaper to go out than to stay at home. And that's exactly what I did. Three dollars a day was just fine for bus fare, but I still needed food and textbooks. Bummer. I already had my own bizarre society-punk social life, a nightlife full of transvestite strippers, transsexuals, rockabilly hustlers, and visiting rock bands. The best thing about visiting rock bands to me was the food that the ass-kissing promoters would provide backstage. With leather thigh boots, a vinyl miniskirt, bleached hair, and a tight starved slim bod, I could get in backstage at just about any rock show. While some of the girls were trying to get in the pants of bands like the Clash, I was trying to sneak off with their untouched crackers and wheels of brie. Once I even managed to get backstage with a visiting Japanese band, the Plastics, who got sushi and rice balls delivered to them.

I had already found out about a swingin' singles club through a girlfriend. We could attend as escorts, drink and snack for free, and even get $30 every time we left with a "member"! The members were all slightly low-rent businessmen, so when I *did* fuck one it was hard to get much takeaway cash. Anyone will buy a willing young girl dinner, a vacation, a line, or a drink . . . as long as she stays with them. But walking-away money was different, and I badly needed to figure out how to get it. Fuck the escargots, slap me a twenty! I felt like screaming in frustration time and again, but the naive college-girl part of me just didn't know how to hustle businessmen for hard cash.

One night I went out on the town in one of the many hot outfits I'd borrowed, slapped together, or snuck out of the local thrift store: a yellow raw silk dress from the '60s, Italian vogue–style, tight across my butt, low cut so the swell of my small tits could burst out, but with enough support so that they stuck up and could be shoved together artificially, the spikiest pumps ever walked on by a human from the sex boutique in London, fishnets, and a black leather double-wrap disco belt with brass buckles to bind me into the outfit even tighter.

When a blonde pretty boy at the after-hours club I was trying to talk my way into said I should be in movies, I wasn't in any position to snub him. I gave the guy my number and hoped he'd call. He had an unusual look for my usual sleazy surroundings: blonde, tanned, dressed like a tennis champ, toting a gym bag, and named Jesse. I was impressed. I'd never been popular in high school, so I'd never fucked a real wholesome-looking man before.

When Jesse called he sounded a little mentally disturbed. He seemed to be having problems with some girl who was a bitch one minute and his girlfriend the next, and a rental car he couldn't afford. He told me he made porn movies. None of this clashed with his tennis pro image in my mind. Since I'd never met a tennis pro or a porn star, it was all unknown territory. He tried to set up a date, but I didn't care. I figured he would just come over to my apartment and fuck me. Sometimes three different men a day might come over and screw me, just by coincidence. They were always guys I liked. I'd usually get dinner, some casually dropped money, an egg roll, whatever.

When Jesse came over, I was dressed in the most slutty outfit I owned: garter belt sticking out of a micro-mini, spike heels, more make-up than any nineteen-year-old should ever need, and a see-through white men's tank top. We got down to business right away. He had a big dick. He ripped off my panties and started matter-of-factly pounding, no adolescent fumbling from him. He kept turning me around like he was almost bored, ramming me from the back doggie-style, hands gripping my tits, slapping my ass, me spread eagle on my bed while he chewed nonchalantly on my pussy, on top of him, on my back again. I was raw and sore but amazed at the same time.

While he fucked, he talked.

"You're nice and tight now, nineteen is a good age. Women lose it when they hit twenty-one, they have to work really hard to stay in shape. They go here, in the thighs, your thighs are nice and tight."

It was more like I was a used car he was examining rather than a thrilled summary of my virtues. He ragged on about some other aspects of his job.

"Some of the women I work with are really disgusting. I'm a star. If I tell the director I just can't fuck a girl, she's out. Dirty loose pussy hanging out on some old broad, girls who don't wash. . . "

For the first time I learned the connection between porn and the underground scene. He knew my runaway cousin, and even had magazines with her looking fat and sad, choking on his dick with her huge mottled tits hanging out. Her former pals, two teensy punk rock sisters, Jerry and Jane, were among his favorite actresses because they could pass for being about twelve, and he could lift them up and throw them around while he was fucking them on film. The same girls who came to punk clubs, who later resided on Clara Street Alley, were also in the now loftily named Adult Business. Need-unwitting stardom.

When he left he offered me $200 to make a porn film with him. Two hundred bucks was an incredible amount of money, and I already knew I wasn't going to be any Miss America. Fucking someone I'd already fucked for free seemed safe. His stunted emotional development and wholesome act made him seem safe. It would have been easier to get emotionally involved with a tree.

On the big day of the filming, we clambered on the train and rode to an out-of-the-way suburb. This was Harold's neighborhood. A chubby, middle-aged guy with glasses let us into his stucco apartment. This was Harold. The first part of the filming was my favorite part, primping. I had latex rubber-look underwear from Woolworth's, a short tight black dress, purple lipstick, spikes, and ratted-out hair. My idea of real cinema glamour.

Jesse wasn't talking to me much by then, and I was sleazily trying to conceal the beginning of a herpes outbreak. For the video loop, I was supposed to be a hooker, he a cowboy customer. He had a cowboy hat to add a fine touch to the believability. He would give me money, and then fuck me, eat me out, and have me suck his dick, which would be so fun that I'd give him back his money at the end.

I wobbled on my spikes while Jesse walked into the scene. I forgot about Harold as he filmed away. I took money from Jesse, and quickly removed my dress. I tried to stay in my latex underwear for a minute because it was new and looked perfect, and I felt it should be recorded on film. Pretty soon I took those off too, though, and we started the scene where Jesse had to eat me out. I had a terrible fear that Jesse would see that I had herpes. I wasn't afraid of giving it to him, I didn't really like him. I was afraid that after all that talk about girls with dirty unwashed pussies, I wouldn't get to make the porn movie, and wouldn't get paid.

He scowled at my cunt and asked if I'd washed, and I quickly said yes. For a frightening moment I thought it was all over, but he probably needed the money as much as I did, so though he looked suspicious, he kept going. I lay on my back on Harold's couch with my cunt pointed at the camera. Jesse spread my lips apart, and then licked my uninfected clit for a close up shot. I started moaning loudly for an overhead mike. I was supposed to moan and groan loudly, but the dialogue wasn't taped.

For the cock-sucking, I ran to the bathroom and redid

the purple lipstick I was convinced made the outfit. I wrapped my lips around Jesse's dick and sucked showily. I sucked him up and down slowly to look sensuous, turned my face up in ecstasy while my mouth was crammed full of cock, and jiggled my tits around.

Finally Jesse got to do what he did best, fuck. I'd never been fucked by anybody who could keep ram-rod hard for any length of time, and on command, and was still a little amazed. He'd told me my cunt was tight when he fucked me at my apartment, but after hours of nonstop pounding I wondered if he'd damaged my resale value a little. He didn't say anything about my tightness during the filming.

I was so used to working hard at minimum-wage jobs, I wanted to do my best to work hard at being in a video loop porn movie. Jesse had said one of the stars he'd worked with would say things like "Fuck my dirty pussy, oh yes, fuck it" to turn him on during filming.

I waited until he was on top and slamming me, moaned loudly, looked ecstatic with my face pointing at the camera, and then exclaimed, "Fuck my dirty bad pussy!" rather loudly. Harold stopped filming, Jesse looked exasperated, and Harold said he could just go ahead and dub it out. Jesse started fucking me again, in a couple of different positions, and I was wet enough to make it easy for him to do me upside down, doggy-style, spread eagle, and riding him in rapid succession.

There was some kind of bizarre charm to this guy. Vietnam Vet, Peevish Porn Star, Preppy Hustler, and Command Cocksman all made for the weirdest package I'd ever met. I was thrilled to get my $200 from Harold, and when he asked me if I knew of any little girls who could just romp around naked, innocently, in his apartment, no harm done, I suppressed a flinch. I got his number and hastily promised to call if any nine-year-olds came to mind.

A surly Jesse took me back to San Francisco on the train. He didn't seem to like me anymore, and I worried for a minute, but knew better than to take it personally. I felt queasy when I thought about Harold and the little girls. Still, I had discovered a horrible and wonderful truth about myself. I was shallow enough to have sex in front of a pervert with a video camera, and not really care.

Feeling like a commodity was kind of fun, and two hundred bucks bought me a lot of food, and at least enough books to keep up in school. I had a hunch that Jesse was just a relatively harmless creep. I never thought he was going to kidnap me, or do me any physical harm. He was too mediocre to be psychotic.

The best thing I got from working at cheap singles clubs, and in porn, is that I know that sometimes people really do have to hustle, and may not choose to spend the rest of their lives sobbing about it. Best of all, thanks to being a permanent part of the cum-soaked backrooms of twenty-four-hour sex shops that still flourish in this land of the Mega Church, I have a fail-safe method of staying away from anything that could really be mentally damaging. I can never hang out with squares. Thank god for smut.

dear john   Mirha-Soleil Ross

Alexandre, Camille, Abel, Sacha, Simon, Raoul, Jean-Pierre, Francois, Mathieu, Angelo, Kwan, Mohamed, Alain, Miguel, Gabriel, Rafael, Eduardo, Kori, Benoit, Thomas, Said, Gilles, Maurice, Albert, Réjean, Cédric, Carmine, Sylvain, Philippe, Carlos . . .

And of course I shouldn't forget Johhhhnnn!

How easy it is to stereotype millions of men when they are all referred to as Johhhhhhn! Might as well call them Dick.

Sexist hypocrites cheating on their wives . . . horny brutes willing to buy women's bodies . . . ugly bogeymen in trench coats objectifying women. . . .

211

In my book: A bunch of mostly nice guys whose invisibility is perhaps the political missing link to the obtainment of prostitutes' rights.

As prostitutes we too often focus on the few bad tricks: the abusive ones who sneak through our screening process, the jerks who set up appointments and never show up, the clumsy twits who squeeze our tits too hard, the ones with cheesy dicks and the foul drunks and the ones who purposely take more time than they paid for to cum. . . . Those make for vivid stories at dinner parties and at performance-art events.

Everyone has heard of clients attacking, raping, murdering prostitutes. The horror stories abound. We're told that the relationships of clients to prostitutes are inherently violent and that they should remained outlawed. Sadly, that mainstream, dominant cultural/political discourse on prostitution is the only representation of the clients of prostitutes that is permitted. In such a context, the voice of the prostitute who dares to object to the false paradigm is the easiest to snuff.

I believe that all men are potentially dangerous and violent, especially within the context of intimate, heterosexual relationships. While a great number of men kill their wives or girlfriends, only a few kill prostitutes. I have had my share of bad tricks. Their violence wasn't born from their "clientness"—what an erroneous concept anyway. Their violence had to do with a set of much more complex factors: coke, crack, heroin, guilt, fear, shame . . . and mostly, it had to do with a cultural, political, legal context created by social workers, police officers, anti–sex work feminists, journalists, and social justice activists—a context within which the work of prostitutes is devalued and seen as a social evil that needs to be eliminated by any means necessary.

This brand of "feminism" has only had an impact on my sweetest clients, making them feel guilty. And it's made me have to spend extra time playing political therapist, having to reassure them that no, they are not hurting my sense of self . . . that if I feel exploited at $150 an hour, I need a serious reality check and that yes, they should continue seeing me 'cause otherwise I'll be stuck with only stinky assholes to sleep with as clients.

I don't know if it is because they stand in such extreme contrast to the way they are portrayed by anti–sex work feminists or some other factor, but there is something in my clients, in their tenderness and gestures towards me, that I find deeply moving.

It's in their voices when they finally get a hold of me on the phone. . . . It's in their smiles when they open the door and invite me in. . . . It's in the sparkles of light I see in their eyes when I say: "First I collect my money and then I tickle your nipples." It's in the way they tense their bodies and hold their breath when I very gently put my lips on those neglected areolas and start sucking on them. . . . It's in their shivering skin when I slowly work my way up to kiss their tight necks. . . . When I start rubbing my body against theirs, it's in these few seconds when it feels like we're suspended in time and they hold on and hold on and hold on as long as they can before finally allowing themselves to release decades of repressed desires. . . . It's in their nervously shaking, moist hands trying to caress me with the intentions of the best lovers. Then it's in their goose bumps and gluttony and giggling and growling and glowing and glory. . . . It is also in less poetic moments when they say things like: "Those are beautiful tits!" while caressing my implants, which actually feel about as delicate as a pair of bowling balls. For the most part, it is in their courage to see me, a transsexual woman, again and again, because yes, in this culture, it takes courage for a man to get so close, so intimate with an individual whom a large percentage of the population considers a freak.

My clients constantly remind me that reclaiming prostitution as a fundamental and legitimate service brings responsibilities. I recently met Claudio, a very attractive, fit, thirty-eight-year-old Italian man, one who had a lovely penis—the kind I like—with enough foreskin to wrap all of next year's holiday season presents. Things were going quite well, we were both enjoying each other but he somehow seemed uncomfortable with his body. At one point he even interrupted our session to take a little break. He wanted to hold me in his arms and caress my hair, but while doing so, I noticed him examining his penis and looking quite perplexed. Just as I thought *Oh no, not another one who wants to know if I find it big enough*, he asked in the most innocent, childlike voice: "Am I circumcised? Because I really don't know."

Whether I am working with a six-hundred-pound disabled man who can't reach his penis to masturbate or an intersex guy whose genitals are nothing like the ones you're used to dealing with or simply the average Joe Blow who wants to start under the blankets cause he's too shy, the men I meet force me to be sensitive to a certain reality: I am not dealing with objects here but with complex and vulnerable individuals who can be stricken by as many body-image problems, self-concept issues, and fears of sexual inadequacy as anyone else.

Some of my clients are married men but it becomes clear when speaking with them that they love their wives, very much enjoy their companionship and, in most cases, want to spend the rest of their lives with them. It's just that sexuality has become limiting, lifeless, or is absent from the relationship. And every so often I meet a man whose dedication to his wife I find particularly commendable.

Anthony is one of them. He started seeing me years after

his wife fell ill due to multiple sclerosis. Every time we'd get together, he would update me on her deteriorating condition and on his struggle trying to keep his family above water; working two jobs in order to afford a private nurse so that his wife wouldn't be locked up in a hospital room for the rest of her life. Last time I saw him he said she was completely incapacitated and no longer cognizant. He told me with tears in his eyes that he saw prostitutes because the idea of seriously dating any woman while his wife was still alive was emotionally unbearable. And *that* I thought brought true meaning to the word "commitment."

Ali is a man I have been seeing for years. He works for minimum wage at the coat check of a restaurant. He's been fighting for over a decade with the Immigration system, spending thousands of dollars in legal fees trying to have his wife—of whom he speaks with so much love—join him here. When I found out how much he was earning an hour and about his costly ordeal with Immigration, I felt concerned, so I told him that maybe he should reconsider spending money to see me. "Don't worry!" he insisted—rightfully offended—adding that it was all budgeted and that all his meager tips were set aside just to see me. "If I didn't spend a few minutes of joy with someone, anyone, nice every couple of months," he concluded abruptly, "I'd probably kill myself!"

Micheal is a man I saw only once. He called me for an

appointment and mentioned that he was sexually inexperienced, that he had been with very few women in his life, never with a transsexual, and that he felt very intimidated. It was a busy day, I was high on Jolt Cola, juggling prostitution with a million chores related to my "political" and "artistic" life, so I said in a sales-pitch tone "I'll be right there to take good care of you." He was a tall, handsome sixty-year-old who spoke and moved with the grace and grounded serenity of James Earl Jones. Our rendezvous unfolded perfectly so before we parted he said "Thank you!" which they always do, so I replied very mechanically "You're welcome!" But he took my hand, held it over his heart; he gave me the sweetest *bisou* on the left cheek and said: "I mean Thank You!" I could tell there was more to this thank you than simple gratitude for activating his vas deferens, so I asked why. He told me that he had been with his wife for forty years, that she had died two years earlier, that he had never been with anyone other than her in all these years and that he thought he'd never again feel at ease being intimate with someone, until he heard my French accent on an escort service line.

These are times when I feel like revolting against this system that is ready to condemn and even jail us for caressing, kissing, and holding each other. . . . These are times when I am able to rid myself of all the fears and anxieties I have about the long-term ramifications of being a prostitute, a social pariah. . . . These are times when I feel like it's worth growing into an old, tired, bitter, dried-up whore. . . . These are times when I feel like there was, indeed, a higher calling for me to sacrifice my personal reputation, comfort, safety, social status, and even my freedom for a greater good.

hello Sister Grimm

Hello, I hope you two are there, or working or something. Oh my god. We've been chasing the dog all through the neighbor's backyard, and the canary escaped! Fred! On top of everything else. I'm up to thirteen now. Thirteen living things in my house! If anyone wants a cat, maybe? There's Max. Or Francesca the parrot. She can say a few things. She says "Hello Kelly." I think she escaped from someone named Kelly. . . . Oh my god, the lizard is crawling up the curtain. Bob! Get the lizard, get it down! . . . About the mop, the house is self-cleaning. Pubic hair on the floor? We've never had that problem before in eighteen years. I'd like to know what you girls are doing over there. . . .

Once I left, I found it difficult to write anything in which I might place Steve, the editor who insisted I was his muse; or Tom, the young divorcé; or Barry, the dirty-talking Southern Baptist who liked to visit early in the morning; or John, the lawyer, who got closer to becoming a friend than most; or Bob, the skinny bottom who would wince at the sight of me; or David, the quiet dean of a local arts school; or the other David, the elderly rabbi; or the drummer of a famous previously punk–now–pop band who gave me all of twenty dollars never to recognize him on the street . . .

I want these fucking guys to start calling. I'm trying to save up for a trip! Tuesday. Fucking slowest day of the week. No one wants a hand job on a Tuesday. You ever notice that? Monday, yeah, bad weekend with the wife or whatever. Thursday, they might start feeling generous, week's almost over, Friday, about to spend another weekend cleaning the garage; but Tuesday, fucking Tuesday.

. . . or the guy whose forty-six-year-old wife was cheating on him with a twentysomething and who really just wanted to talk (I asked why he wasn't seeing a shrink; he told me he didn't care for the stigma); or Mark, who cried silently as

I listened (his wife had died in a car accident); or Trey, who wanted to save me because I seemed sad; or Larry, who drove a taxi and smoked way too much pot and told all the girls he loved them; or the girls, the ones I cared about, the ones I fought with; or what it feels like to have the curtains drawn all day, as you sit in your lingerie with your feet perched on the heater, listening to Adrienne's troubles, wondering if the phones will ever ring . . .

I had this dream that I was walking down a street in a place I've never been, and yet it's familiar. And I find a huge dead yellow bird lying in the middle of the road. And in the dream it's my birthday. It was a present.

. . . or the blue candleholders; or the faulty washing machines which left the towels smelling vaguely of cum; or the "self-cleaning" house where I worked and the crazed madam who had a penchant for saving strays, but who refused to buy us a mop; or the actual mop I bought with my own money; or how I diligently mopped the whole place topless as Claire watched from behind her newspaper; or Claire, who cooked the best vegetarian meals while I narrated daytime television shows from the other room; or the way it tore my girlfriend up that I gave all I had to strangers and left none for her . . .

I was thinking of writing a medical book called Hand Jobs: How I Got Carpal Tunnel, *and filling it with a bunch of short stories completely unrelated to the title.*

. . . or Christine's boyfriend, who thought she was leaving home each morning to work at a jewelry store; or Brielle, who looked like a midwestern cheerleader and scolded me one day for wearing my Skivvies into a session, and who bought into some kind of conspiracy theory which compelled her to shoot guns in the woods every weekend, in case "they" were coming to get "us" (I was never sure who "they" were, but I was pretty certain that I was not included in her version of "us"); or Brian, the wealthy Republican, who volunteered at the local animal shelter and cried when they euthanized his favorite pit bull; or John, the very tall, very quiet poker player who would come to see me after every big win . . .

Stanley broke his leg in the backyard when I was chasing him! Why is the answering machine on? Is anyone there? . . . I just talked to Emma two minutes ago. What is going on over there? Well, you two better be in session. Do you hear me? . . . Bob! Don't carry him like that, don't you know what kind of pain he's in? . . . Is anyone there? Brielle, are you there? Well if you need me, I'll be at the . . . Bob! Show some humanity for Christ's sake . . . his leg is dangling! Okay, well, just so you know, Mary's client broke a table last week. And if anyone else breaks a table over there . . . Stanley, oh my god . . . well, I am not paying for it, is all!

. . . or Mary, whose client broke the table; or how no one ever answered the phone when Margaret called to "check in" and how her phone calls always reminded me of an NPR version of Animal Cops; or how we were responsible for putting a spell on her boyfriend by having a certain set of candles lit at all times or else; or how her husband Bob brought me some unbelievably bad lesbian porn so that I could examine the authenticity of the sex; or how I neither wanted to burst his bubble nor clue him into my world and told him "this is exactly how lesbians have sex" . . .

There is a serious gas leak over here. It's giving me a migraine. Can you please send someone? Yes, I cannot work like this. You know I'm already dealing with my candida right now and I'm really just trying to make it through my cleanse.

. . . or how Samantha got the shits when she was on a three-week raw food diet and could not work, but came in anyway and slept all day on the huge, leopard-print couch; or how we consulted the tarot one day to investigate whether we were being watched by the cops and though neither one of us really knew how to interpret the tarot, we managed to determine that we were on the precipice of a preemptive catastrophe (which never happened); or how Mary just didn't come into work one day because she decided to move to Ohio to become a teacher and how I was going to follow her example, but just kept on folding pink towels . . .

Did you know that colonies of birds, just before they are ready to migrate, get really quiet. They call that "dread." And penguins carry their eggs on their feet. Did you know that? There is no way to really carry eggs on a pair of red hooker boots, is there?

. . . or Diane, who dreamt of having an office job equipped with a desk, which would serve as the resting place for a framed picture of her daughter; or Lynn, who had been on the "Geek to Sleek" *Ricki Lake Show* and thought everything the clients had to offer was "chump change;" or the hippie house I worked for where the girls set up a gigantic altar in the middle of everything and were constantly creating "sacred space;" or how once the curtains caught on fire, because Lily and I were trying to sage the "negative energy" off of each other; or how the very next week Stuart, the owner, closed it all down because he could no longer afford the liability we had become.

anacam Ana Voog

Ana Voog was the second ever 24/7 home webcam on the Internet, starting in the fall of 1997. Today she is the net's longest running cam. Her site has included a daily journal, a 30-second-refresh cam picture, chat rooms, bulletin boards, email lists, endless photo archives, and at times a mobile cam that she takes out into the world. It quickly snowballed from a small experiment to a site with thousands of members worldwide and a busy online community centered around her cam. Following are screenshots and excerpts from the journal (called ANAlog) she kept during the first year and a half she had the cam, at a time when the whole world was trying to figure out what the technology meant.

SEPTEMBER 4, 1997

i've decided to write journal entries about my webcamness wrrrld. this is my 1st ANAlog. i've been on the net now for a week. it's a freaky and cool thing! i don't know if i should pay attention to the cam or not. today i'm not because i just need a break and to finally get caught up on some email. and my house is going to the pits! i have so much laundry and dishes to do! eek! i can't even get connected to my temperamental server now anyway. i keep crashing every now and then.

after the 1st 4 days of being on cam, i went on vacation for a week, and it was so weird 'cause for the first few days of trying to unwind i kept seeing the monitor of myself in my head as i'd try to go to sleep. it was so crazy. y'know how things get all surreal and thoughts make no sense right when you're on the verge of sleep? well, i was pulling down menus for my thoughts! and i was moving pictures over in my mind with a cursor and resizing them! i'd go out to dinner and all i could think of is "wow, that ketchup bottle would make a good cam shot!" or "too bad i don't have the cam to show how the light is hitting those rotating pies in that display case!"

i hope after awhile these thoughts will just settle down. the technology of all of this is so astounding, mindblowing, yet so incredibly archaic at the same time. people staring at computers all over the world waiting for minutes for a picture to refresh. it's endearing and insane. i like it. i'm glad to be a part of this whatever-it-is.

it's eerie to sleep with the cam on you. i'll wake up and see it shining and blinking at me and it's like a dream.

SEPTEMBER 7, 1997

3:40am, wow, it's cool to take a shower and not worry about what picture the cam is going to snap of you! it's a completely different vibe having the cam off. aaaah, my "old" life! someday i might get used to the camera and just forget it's there, but not yet! i still feel pretty self-conscious. i wake up and put on lipstick right away or else i look so washed out.

it sure is quieter in here with one computer shut off, too. i find it interesting that so many of you want to watch me sleep. i sort of feel like you're all watching over me, protecting me.

i really want to get a cam in every room. and be able to take the cam outside with me. i think it would be just hilarious if people saw me do absolutely everything. it would be so over-the-top and ridiculous. it's kind of like i live in a "cam-cage." my house is getting messier and messier.

SEPTEMBER 10, 1997

i haven't gone outside in days because of my weird schedule and this cam. i hope i make it outside tomorrow for awhile. i really want to lie on the grass. oh, man, just thinking about it, i could cry!

and before i go to sleep, i have one last request, will SOMEONE PLEASE TELL ADAM ANT TO CALL ME? IT'S IMPORTANT!

SEPTEMBER 13, 1997

i'm glad i started some controversy over the "pussy causes war" pix. i'm finding this cam a very powerful medium to reach a lot of people in trying to demystify the body of at least ONE woman! i want to try on every female stereotype and archetype and shatter them all.

and i want to do this in a humorous, fun and real way. i am still just at the beginning stages of exploring this medium and searching for what i'm "trying to say." perhaps what i'll say will be an accident. done in some small menial thing i do. i don't know. i just want to break down barriers of all kinds, race, sex, time zones, countries, morals, rules, language, etc. etc. etc.

SEPTEMBER 17, 1997

i'm feeling a bit overwhelmed with everything at the moment. it will pass, but in this moment. . .augh.

trying to find where i fit into to the webcam. all of a sudden i am so close to me that i cannot see myself anymore. my life blurs into entertainment, and i wonder if my microwaved dinner is entertaining enough. i don't know when i can just be selfish and not think about the cam. i think about the lighting, when is the best time to take a shower. i feel guilty if i sleep all day because people will think badly of me. and it's hard when you look or feel like shit to be on cam. if i don't do something interesting i feel i'm letting you all down. if i get too down, i feel like i'm letting you down.

SEPTEMBER 28, 1997

a lot of people worry about me that i am so antisocial. but i am just that way. and i like it that way. i think i'm getting more and more antisocial all the time, which is pretty ironic since i'm communicating with more people now than i ever have communicated with before.

it's been very very windy the last few days and it gets me a bit excited 'cause i know then that change is coming. weather to me is always very symbolic, but in a very literal way. as is everything to me.

OCTOBER 3, 1997

i'm noticing that a big issue that is crawling under the surface of this live cam thing is CONTROL. some people like the fact that they have no control over my life, they seem to like the aspect that they don't know what will happen next. but some people go BERSERK over the smallest thing like my lighting. they say "move this way, move that way, your lighting is too bright i can't see you, your lighting is too dark i can't see you, your hair is messy, is that all i'm going to see? you are always asleep! you never sleep! why don't you smile? wave at me, change your caption!"

OCTOBER 7, 1997

my cam has turned black and white due to the fact that i'm frying it by leaving it on 24/7. i think if i turned it off then turned it back on again it would go back to color. but i'm enjoying the black and white. i did some groovy "film noir pin-up" stuff the other night

OCTOBER 8, 1997

some changes have happened in the chatroom because of trolls coming in there and wrecking it for everyone. and i'm just drained from it and it's distracting me from my life and my happiness. 1st of all the chatroom called #anacam is now a place where only i can speak and everyone else cannot speak. think of it as a radio of sorts where i can broadcast in my thoughts as i'm thinking them. and you can listen but i can't hear you. it's much more peaceful for me this way. for those that wish to speak there is #analove (where you go to talk about happy things) and there is #anaslam (where you go to bitch about stuff).

i'm #1 on Kat's Kam Konnections again. woo woo! i think 'cause maybe i was cleaning the cat poop off the floor in the nude.

AnaFone cards will be available starting Friday October 10. you can call and talk to me directly. The following denominations are available:

$6 for 3 minutes
$10 for 5 minutes
$20 for 10 minutes
$50 for 25 minutes

NOVEMBER 21, 1997
i've been writing in my new bulletin board (bbs) so much that i've neglected writing a new ANAlog. the bbs has been

AMAZING and chaotic. it received over 500 posts from around the world in the 1st few hours it had opened! WOW! and it's been fun in there, and intense, and angry, and gleeful, and just about every emotion with a myriad of subjects from the war against women to pimento loaf. from alien abductions to depression to sex with midgets. it's been insane. even god has posted many times!

NOVEMBER 25, 1997

EXPLOITATION? ya, that's just it, i'm just "exploiting" myself SO much that there is just no way anyone could exploit it further. i just want to take it BEYOND the point of exploitation so that it all becomes a great big joke on "the exploiter" and therefore it cannot even exist anymore. i mean, there IS something really funny here, like it's all getting turned inside out. and i can post here about "them," the exploiters. whatever "they" do to me, is done to them. because i'm live 24/7, any way they affect me, anything they do, is reflected right back at them via my cam, via the net, via posts. there's nowhere u can hide anymore. the net is just a symbol that we are a telepathic race. that we are all pulled into this together.

NOVEMBER 30, 1997

many times when i am just blankly staring at nothing it seems, i am in fact listening to such nice music, i am surfing the net and looking at fabulous things, i am talking on the phone to all my friends. i have people over ALL THE TIME and you do not even know! because some people that come over don't wish to be on cam. keep in mind you are only seeing 120 split seconds of my life per hour. and this is from one narrow camera angle, without sound. i have a whole house and much goes on. i try to convey as much as i can, but the medium is limited, as is language. all you can do is speculate about me.

i have lived as this person now for 31 years. this cam has been on only for a few months. i worked very very hard to get where i am now. i worked in many factories, as a house-keeper in hospitals, as a stripper, dancing 14 hours a day in high-heeled shoes. most of my life i have worked for mini-mum wage. i have done hard labor and pushed heavy things around in big dusty factories for $4 an hour, i have washed the floors of many a place, i have cleaned up the puke and urine and blood of sick people. 120 seconds per hour is mere-ly a peek into a much bigger life.

DECEMBER 7, 1997

i was interviewed by a music 'zine called CAKE and they took my picture, too. there is a link to CAKE in the ANArchives. i'm excited to see how it will turn out. whenever i give someone an interview, i don't know how they will choose to interpret what was said. sometimes my sentences are taken completely out-of-context. i also took my picture for a german magazine called MAX. i am REALLY excited about that! woo! AND the coolest thing of all is that a very big german computer magazine called KONR@D voted me #1 most interesting site on the net!

JANUARY 2, 1998

my 1st ANAlog of the new year! my new year's eve was sure better than xmas, i can tell u that! xmas couldn't have sucked more. i went to my mom's and she just freeeeeeeeeeked on me about the cam saying that my life is more destructive than if i were shooting heroin, and i'm a prostitute, and it's like i'm dead to her now. so . . . ok. i cried and stayed in a room with pooka. it was just a terrible xmas. and that's all i have to say about that.

there was a little article on me in *The New York Post*

and i found out that Willian Gibson, author of "neuromancer" (he also coined the term "cyberspace"!) watches me from time to time!

FEBRUARY 11, 1998

well, i called my dad today. he is a lutheran minister from a small town. the local paper here that reaches across this state made it to my dad. and he is not pleased, to say the least. in fact, i have never heard him so displeased with me since i quit high school.

last night i dreamt that i pushed the button that sent a bomb to china to blow it up. this bomb went straight through the earth leaving a hole, which caused 1/2 the earth to flood and the other 1/2 to dry up. i wandered the earth looking for shelter and trying to gather a few of my belongings to save. i came across my water-logged stuffed animals and started to cry because i thought they were dead. but i wrung the water out of them and got them back into shape and tried to sew them to my jacket so that i could carry them around with me that way, but i had no thread, only a needle.

i also got an email from my old sunday school teacher that contained a picture that i couldn't decipher and it said " i am disappointed but i'm not surprised" which i thought was really really mean. was he saying that he is not surprised that i am disappointing? i wonder what the picture was. and if he is so upset, why is he watching me?

FEBRUARY 27, 1998
so it's hard for me to convey what goes on with me right now. i am sick of explaining myself and talking about myself and looking at myself.

i just feel poked and prodded. film crews, interviews, inter-rogations. all screaming at me "are you valid?" how can a big fake-titted bleach-blonde so-called faerie queen x-stripper cam grrl net "porn star" call herself an artist?

in trying to get together my thesis on my validity and value . . . i have ignored myself, and my household and am finding myself rather depressed.

MARCH 10, 1998

pleez help keep anacam up and running by becoming a member of ana2!!! and thank u ana2 members for being such a great support! u r truly a pleasure 2 interact with !

i'm having spring fever in the worst way. being stuck in this tiny apartment in snow with cams on . . . is it the 3rd already? or is it the 2nd? i can't even believe it's march! next month is my birthday, on april 18 i'll be 32!

btw, i don't think i'm schizophrenic if i define myself.

to those who asked, my 9mm is a tokarov made in china. i guess it's not a very good gun. i don't know, it was my first one. the .38 special is a Wesson thing, i think. all i know is they shoot, and that's good enough 4 me right now . . . but i really have to learn more about them and how to clean them and stuff. like my song says, "and could u send me sum money money money, i'm out of ammunition . . . "

MARCH 17, 1998

maybe i'm letting too much information seep into my life. but, it's two-way . . . i can't stop reading those damn bbs because i'm so curious as to what rotten things they will say about me next. it's a strange addiction!

there is an article on me in the online-edition of DER SPIEGEL. and i did an interview with a freelance writer for penthouse. She was doing a piece on webcams, not just me.

i just woke up from a dream that i was in a ufo and i brought my cordless phone with and it still worked way above the city of new york. i tried to get them to fly past my friend's window. i had another dream that i was singing this fantastic song that was very "dead can dance"-ish and diamanda galas came up and congratulated me on my fine singing. then i used her bathroom on the plane.

i dream about famous people a lot. i think i must have dreamed about every famous person by now. most times i am comforting them for some reason.

i barely even have time to write this ANAlog! aaaa!!!! i'm getting so super busy now with my music! i'm going to be playing in las vegas in the middle of may. and other tentative cities are san francisco, los angeles, new york, and philadelphia
. . . i'll let you know any details as soon as i know them!

also, i'm going to be appearing on a variety show called VIBE
on UPN (hosted by sinbad). can life get weirder? i'll be singing
on this show . . . and it might be happening in as soon as two
weeks! i have SO much to do, it's insane. i have to pull this
all together and practice my ass off! so, that's what i've been
doing and why i haven't been home much or if you see me
home, i'm typing or on the phone . . .

i'm trying to figure out how to bring my cam with to all of
these things . . . and eventually this WILL happen. so hang
on to your hats for some bizarre adventures! my life is in
transition . . . therefore, so is anacam . . .

ummm, what else . . . oh ya . . . i was in USA Today magazine . . .
on thursday or friday . . . it had a big picture of me . . . but i
still haven't even had time to find a copy!

MAY 12, 1998

I got interviewed on E! for an hour long special they are doing on "women of the web." so i had to get my make-up on and sit very still under these bright lights while trying to be as coherent as possible. my mouth was all dry and my lipstick was too glossy, but i think i made it through. i got to do one of those E! ID things . . . i had to say "if it's happening in entertainment, it's happening on E!" (this was an extremely funny thing for me to say, if you are decadent enough to get that little drug joke there.)

JULY 26, 1998

i went to new york last week for a party that yahoo/intel had. I did a heck of a lot of interviews for magazines and stuff. i met so many people that i didn't get to have any "real" conversations. who interviewed me? i wish i could remember! i do remember that i did something for electronic musician, vh1, details, and . . . 10 other things.

i made some pretty cool pix when i was in new york . . . you can see some of them in "arcana." that was when i had the most fun . . . when i'd return to my hotel and play with my cam. i missed my boyfriend a lot, even though i was gone only 2 days . . . so i took an earlier flight home. then the plane got stuck on the runway and we had to get towed back to the airport. i turned my cam on in the plane and left a message of my plight! funnily enough, after all my interviews, a reporter from the new york times approached me as we transferred planes. she said that she had noticed my shirt which i had written across it in permanent marker "yes, they're fake." she was going to do a story on the increasing popularity of breast implants . . . so i sat by her on the way home and gave her my story.

we had a great conversation about new mexico and the strange flash floods, too. and how this one place is so quiet that u can hear the sound of a bird flapping its wings overhead, if one passes by above u! i so much want to experience that kind of silence. i've never been to a desert, and i want to visit them all. i want books about them, photographs of them, aerial photographs especially! i was totally taken by the look of the desert between las vegas and los angeles, so much that it brought tears to my eyes!

but back to the new york times . . . so that article ran a few days ago. i now have this quote to add to my resume: "Ms. Voog's breasts are round, high and firm looking."—the new york times

SEPTEMBER 14, 1998

WHAT DOES "GRACE" MEAN TO YOU???

OCTOBER 28, 1998

right now i'm in the middle of "all nude all week" week. i'm
on day 3! i just did it spur of the moment as just a funny
thing to do to celebrate "the harvest." thank god it's been
an unusually warm week for october. i guess i just wanted
to see if i could even go a whole week without wearing
clothes . . . and it's actually hard to do! now, on day three,
i'm starting to feel a bit overexposed, i'm missing that nice
cocoon feeling of clothing! my skin isn't used to feeling everything all the time! i wonder if by day 7 i'll start curling
up like an armadillo?

DECEMBER 16, 1998

on the anacam page, jason put up a link to a rating site called
"camdepot" that so far today was bringing in 150 new people
to my site. i don't know how i feel about that . . . "voting"
and "being ranked." of course, everyone likes it if they're the
most popular, and i definitely like new people to find my site
. . . i've decided to keep the link up for now at least to see if
anything comes of it . . . or something. i went to the page
and it seems pretty nice. some guy listed on there has a ferret
cam and that's cool.

my stripper year
Stephen Elliott

First there was Toni in his spar-
kling cocktail dress, serving
drinks at Neo on Clark Street. The bar was dark, there were
no windows, only a blue-lit clock. Toni had thin legs covered
in track marks beneath his fishnet stockings. He brought me
elegant-looking drinks on a silver tray. I hid in the corners
or in the middle of the dance floor. I went to Neo alone and
Toni sensed my loneliness and wanted to mother me to health
but it didn't happen. Toni died at three in the morning in a
stranger's apartment in Humboldt Park lying next to a broken
needle, blood streaming from his nose, emerald skirt riding

in waves across his hips, tights ripped, a slipper dangling from his toe, eyes wide open.

Then there was Toni's friend Tony. Tony worked at Berlin, had tribal tattoos covering half his body, long, thick black hair like a horse's mane, and every year the free weekly paper voted him best bartender in the city.

I had friends but they were sleeping, and they weren't real friends. Tony didn't charge me for drinks either and I hovered near his bar, an oasis next to the entrance. I danced close to Tony. I never wanted to go home. I said, "What kind of boys do you like?" and he said, "Straight boys," and I smiled.

Tony had a fashion show and I walked the runway at Berlin in striped shorts with thin straps over my shoulders. There were so many people there, all of them high on pills, dehydrated, and watching. I danced slowly past them. It was like being perfect, which is always an illusion. I was followed by a man in a straw hat, his gown covered in pale green bulbs. "Do you have any more swimsuits?" I asked Tony. "I want to go again."

"You are so vain," he said, patting my ass. I gave him a quick, sly kiss on the lips, before climbing back on the stage.

It was my stripper year. My heroin year. I danced Thursday nights at Berlin. Two sets, three songs, free whiskey, $75, occasional tips. They called me a go-go boy but I was really just decoration, cheap art. I scored heroin on the west side, piloting my giant car through the burnt-out landscape, home of the '68 riots, the stained remnants of an assassination in Tennessee, the empty lots like broken teeth. Trash and parts everywhere, pipes protruding from the rubble, chassis on cinder blocks, men in lawn chairs on corners in front of vacant three flats. I got robbed. I got beat up. Things weren't going well. Nothing made sense. I was having the best time of my life.

I didn't make enough money on a podium at Berlin. I danced at the Lucky Horseshoe, a front for prostitutes on Halsted Street. We weren't allowed to sit between sets. We had to mingle with clients at the bar. "They like it when you pay attention," the owner told us. "Open seats are for customers."

So we would stand and they would sit. I met a man who bred dogs. He stuck $5 in my thongs after my first dance. "It's like selling people," he said, laying a rough hand on my waist. "Only it's dogs, so it's legal." Then he let out a monstrous laugh.

The going rate was $20 a day plus tips. The going rate was $80 for a blow job down at the Ram, a dirty theater with private booths six painted steps below street level a block away. There were sugar daddies who came to the Horseshoe but it was up to you to parse them from the fakers and dreamers. They said, "What do you want to do with your life? I can help you." If you were a writer they were an agent. If you were an actor they were a director, a producer. If you wanted to go to school they would give you a place to stay while you got your act together. They knew someone on the admissions board. The clients at the Horseshoe were whatever you might need. But I needed to be found attractive. I needed to be loved unconditionally. And I was very angry about something.

I had a college degree.

This is all true.

It was 1995, the hottest summer on record, or so somebody told me at the time. It's a fact I've never bothered to check. They were carrying dead seniors by the dozen in a phalanx of stretchers from the nursing homes on Touhy Avenue. I lived in a squat above a garage a bullet away from the project buildings. I could make out the top of the Sears Tower from my porch. I had a roommate and during the day we would go to the slab along North Avenue Beach and lie there like seals, diving into the water every twenty minutes or so until the sun went down. We lay on the warm concrete watching the sunset and then the stars. "Life is good," he said.

Sunday afternoons I danced between films at the Bijou. Twenty minutes of porn then one boy on the stage, one boy in the audience. The men pulled their penises out, stroking themselves, sliding a dollar in my pants with their free hand. The Bijou smelled of bleach. I climbed over the seats barefoot.

I was like a spider, crawling along armrests and chair backs, never touching the ground. I stayed away from the older men. They had been around too long. They were looking for a good deal. I paid special attention to a fat boy who sat in the second row. He was probably my age. His hair was flaxen and I worried that nobody loved him the most. I was projecting my own feelings. I sat on his lap, squeezed his shoulder, kissed his neck. I wanted to be capable of loving him for more than a few minutes but I wasn't. He gave me a dollar and I hugged him, pulling his nose against my naked chest. "It's okay," I said.

There were rooms above the Bijou. Offices, a movie studio. The manager kept a picture of me in his desk drawer. He asked me to act in a bisexual porn movie. I said I didn't mind. I was put in a room and given five minutes to get a hard on. This was my audition. The room was giant and empty with slanted beams holding up the roof and great windows looking across Old Town. I jerked off, paging casually through the porn next to the bed. The director burst in with a Polaroid camera. "Yes," he exclaimed when he saw my hard-on.

The pay was $300. I was told it was very important to be nice to the woman. She was a queen. I wanted the money but I was ambivalent about the film. What I really wanted was to be tied up. I wanted to be humiliated on tape. I wanted women with strap-ons to grip me by the throat and slide inside of me.

I wanted to be wrapped in cellophane, like a present, unable to move. That was the kind of film I wanted to be in. But I didn't know how to say that at the time and people who don't know how to ask rarely get what they want.

I danced at the Manhole on lights-out night. I was four feet above the floor on a square pedestal. I had to be careful not to step over the edge. Hands came from everywhere, palms stretching below my balls, fingers trying to find my asshole. I couldn't see past the elbows.

"Stop it," I said softly. The music was so loud, nobody heard me.

It was my heroin year. I shot bags next to the couch and slept on the living room floor. I missed a night at Berlin. Then I missed another one. Summer was over. We stopped going to the beach. It got darker earlier. It was almost Thanksgiving. I dated Stacey, a Barbie-doll stripper with a bad coke habit and implants that didn't take, they felt like twelve inch softballs inside her breasts. She made $400 a shift. She knew about bars in Cicero that never closed. She crashed her car and the barmaid asked if she spilled her drink. Her other boyfriend was a police officer. "He's very violent," she told me. "He wants to put his gun in your mouth and ask you some questions. He broke the lock on my door. Do you want to come over?"

After Stacey I dated Zahava. Zahava came from a good Southern family. She had been a pom-pom girl. She had been to finishing school. It seemed like she was always happy. She was the only person I knew with good posture. She wanted me to go to law school. I turned her on to heroin. Years later she would tell me I was the first bad thing that ever happened to her. Zahava said I was handsome. I told her when you're a stripper you don't worry about your appearance. You always feel attractive when people are willing to pay to see you naked. It was the biggest lie I ever told. I stared at the other strippers, the bricks in their stomachs, trapezoids like baby mountains. It made me nauseous to think about. I wasn't good enough looking to dance at the Vortex but they let me in for free. I was low-rent and I knew it. I had an eating disorder and long hair. The only advantage I had over anybody was that I knew how to dance.

I never made the movie. I was in a small room with dark wood floors on top of a big house in Evanston near the lake. I took a hotshot and passed out with blood streaming from my nose and foam gurgling at my mouth. Just like Toni a year earlier. My friend turned me over so I wouldn't choke on my own vomit, then he left me to die.

But I didn't die. Firemen came the next day. They were strong and good. They strapped me to a chair, carried me down three flights of stairs. "Where's your family?" the owner of the house asked as they hauled me past her. "What's your parents' phone number?" I didn't tell her. It was the first good decision I made that year. I was paralyzed for eight days and the nurses let me piss all over myself. When I was discharged from the hospital I walked with a limp. I told people I fell down a flight of stairs. Eventually the limp went away but it took time. And it took time to learn how to eat. I lost thirty pounds.

I didn't strip again. Or shoot heroin. I got a master's degree. I moved to a ski resort and the customers would sit at the bar unbundling their scarves. I wore black pants, a white shirt, and a patterned vest like all the other employees. We looked like dancing monkeys. Every day someone would stare at the mountains while I refilled their cup. "I wish I could trade places with you," they would say, maybe dropping a dollar into the plastic pitcher sitting empty on the counter's edge.

songs Vaginal Davis

Everyone wants to be able to sing along to the new songs I've written with my Berlin-based, proto-Marxist, post-politikal art rock band Ruth Fischer. Ruth Fischer was the famed feminist forerunner, and head of the German Communist Party of the 1920s. This new project began late 2005, and is a supergroup collaboration between me and the members of the German art kollective Cheap, and the Albanian folk group The Super 700s.

PRESENT PENICATIVE

LYRICS BY VAGINAL DAVIS

The shakiest gun in the west

dammit

the shakiest gun in the west

with that limp limp wrist

he is a meek dentist

to fight oral ignorance

dammit

smut and moral corruption

spewed forth like garbage

from the lecherous, vile,

lewd and licentious

mind of a child

filthy little d

de-generate.

Dammit

the shakiest gun in the west

the shakiest gun in the west

Look at his face—the face of a smut-monger.

Look at his body

wasted away by the dissipation

and debauchery

life of unspeakable depravity

alienating, superficial conformist.

distinct individual flamboyance

invisible art culture influence

notions of sexual liberation, anti-authoritarian

    behavior,

expression of indifference,

from the shakiest gun in the west

expressions of indifference

the shakiest gun in the west

reduced the gay political agenda to doctrinaire slogan-
eering and politically correct rhetoric which resulted
in an anti-intellectual, anti-dialectical ontology,

ambivalence and paradox had heretofore been one of
our most effective strategies.

a stratification of the sexes

individual style, radical politics, and anarchic
behavior—the very tenets of homosexual radical-
ism

politically it was also attempting to rethink how to organize society, to decentralize power and to fight corporatization.

The early roots of punk were also based on sexual revolution: experimentation with sexual ambivalence, bi- and homosexuality, androgyny, and even gender dysphoria

disposable or worthy of contempt even while adoring you.

ABSORBINE GYLLENHAUL

LYRICS BY VAGINAL DAVIS

Chorus

Jake Gyllenhaul

I can always tell when he's near me

Jake wants it all wants it all wants it all

Jake Gyllenhaul

can't control himself when he's near me

Jake, wants it all

wants it all

wants it all

I know I shouldn't keep him waiting

With those eyes that kill me

and are so penetrating

and his body fills me

from the ejaculating

and I give it all

give all give it all

give it all

(repeat chorus)

I don't know what he sees in me

I'm not Scandinavian royalty

he's the hot boy of the Hollywood town

he's the young one who can carry the crown

I'll get up for him and then lie back down

give it all

give it all give it all

give it all

THE MALADJUSTED RULE

LYRICS BY VAGINAL DAVIS

chavs chavettes

chavestites (repeat as chant)

the maladjusted rule (repeat as chant)

fool

from that you can construe

tool

if you're mindlessly content

you are just a slug, inert, a dent

you do not move the human race forward

yours is the face you can't go towards

I scream to see you take up so much space

the outsiders should rule the race

chavs chavettes

chavestites (repeat as chant)

the maladjusted rule (repeat as chant)

fool

from that you can construe

tool

Take the trauma of youth

use as a creative bridge

its all about perspective

the popular they peak too early

I much prefer the sour and surly

thank you for the misfit

thank you sweet misfit

harassed and tortured

individualists

(shouting)

the city and the pillar

nobody knows my name

other voices, other rooms

play it as it lays

the history of forgetting

the poetry of william blake

michelangelo, dante, keats

caravaggio

turning trauma into creativity that's why the maladjusted rule!!!

house call
Aiden Shaw

The john invited me in. He fell back against the wall, then collecting himself said, "Follow me." The stairway led to a living room with red carpet. This room was well lit and made the carpet look very bright, almost throbbing. It seemed to pour over the top step on its way downstairs. I glanced around the room, checking out the place. When entering this kind of situation, I become very wary. Everything becomes a clue as to who it is I'm dealing with. Clear plastic podiums sat spaced at intervals around the edge of the room. On them were gold, black, and white ceramic figures: the front view of a muscular torso, the back view including buttocks, and a pair of women's hands. There was a single print on each wall, behind glass and framed in bright red plastic. I hadn't seen prints like these since the early '80s. They were all of women, wearing wide-brimmed hats and red lipstick. The first was smoking a cigarette from a long holder; the second was wearing long black gloves and appeared to be straightening her hat; the third was blowing a kiss; and the fourth had long red nails which were laced together, supporting her chin. I was surrounded.

Proudly, he took me on a tour, tripping, stumbling, and holding himself against walls for support. I was shown his bedroom. The walls and ceiling, although covered with textured wallpaper, were both painted with black gloss. The cupboard doors entirely covering one wall and a shelf running the length of another all got the same treatment. On the shelf I could make out a plastic figure of Jesus beside what looked like a bible. Black carpet started at the doorway and had a chrome strip to cover the join. Several screws were missing and it bulged in the middle. The door was stopped open by a brick. I presumed the whole floor was covered with this black carpet but I could only see it in patches, through the bunches of unwashed smelling clothes.

The bed sheets had probably once been black, but over time had faded to gray. From the ceiling hung the wire frame of a lampshade with a dusty red scarf draped over it. Beside this, directly over the bed, was a sling with chains too thin to really support anybody. From the doorway I could just see under the edge of the bed. There were several pillowcases, the same color as the ones on the bed, apparently stuffed with more clothes. Maybe these were the smelly ones and the scattered ones were clean. I could also see, spilling out from the other end of the bed a few superhero comics, a porn magazine, and a stray cock ring.

We moved on, back through the living room and into the kitchen. Where the red carpet stopped, cream patterned linoleum took over. This room clearly didn't have the same aesthetic as the other rooms, and I guessed it hadn't been decorated since he'd moved in. Maybe he thought it didn't count. It was like a million kitchens I'd seen worldwide, with the obligatory gray/cream color scheme. I think it wasn't actually meant to be part of the tour, but was included so he could top up his drink. He got this from a selection of bottles beside a microwave. The fridge had three magnets on it: a Dalmatian, a glitter-covered pair of ruby slippers, and what looked like pink neon swirling handwriting. I think it was the word Fabulous. Tucked under this was a note that read "call mum."

There were cupboards but they barely registered as distinct from the wall behind them or anything else in the room. The handles were brass-looking disks, like miniature versions of a door handle you might find in a castle. The nerve center of this room appeared to be a glass fruit bowl area. In it were four brown bananas, small change, a comb, a stick of chewing gum, and a notebook. Behind this, propped on the marbled Formica counter, was a bulletin board covered in pictures of glamorous women, porn stars, and polaroids of men (whom I guessed were previous prostitutes he'd hired), mounted like animal head trophies. The john took my arm and led me back through the living room again and into an adjoining bathroom.

"This is my favorite," he said, turning and winking at me. "If you know what I mean." I didn't. The wall tiles, carpet, wicker wash basket, and soap were all shades of black. The only things in the room that weren't black were the red plastic marble-effect bath and some off-white socks and underpants on the floor by the wash basket.

"Check out the sexy ceiling," he slurred, trying to gesture but sloshing his drink and falling against the doorframe. I looked up, seeing my reflection and behind me, a hand with a glass in it. I smiled at myself. "We'll get in there later . . . " he said, referring to the bath. I glanced over at it and noticed several brown marks where the plastic had melted. Cigarette burns, I guessed. "I'll soap you up."

"That'll be great," I said, my eyes flicking to the soap. It hung from the faucet by a black piece of rope. Again he took my arm, more as support for himself than as a guide for me. He pointed haphazardly to a chrome and glass coffee table.

"There's some coke there if you want it."

"Thanks." I knelt down to do some, but was distracted by a bowl of chocolates in colorful, shiny wrapping on top of the table, then, through the glass, at things under the table. There was a slipper upside down with a foil milk bottle top stuck to the sole. Also there was some mail that hadn't been opened. I couldn't remember the john's name, but I knew it didn't correspond to the one on the mail.

"Don't worry there's plenty more," he said, presumably thinking I was staring at the coke.

"Right!"

"Help yourself to chocolate too. Sit down. Let me get you a drink. Whiskey okay?"

"Great!" He went to the kitchen.

I couldn't see a cat, but the couch was covered in hairs. I realized there was an animal smell to the whole place. It was only a minute or two before he returned. The curtains were dark green, made from a synthetic velvety fabric. The TV was probably the biggest you could get, five years ago. It already looked dated. There were birthday cards on top. Most had cartoon characters or beautiful naked men on them. It must be his birthday. I looked around for more evidence of this, but there wasn't any. The TV might have been the designated area for birthday. Every other surface was covered with something. A figurine, a photo in Perspex frame, a cuddly toy, or glass something.

"So what did you have in mind?" I asked, with innuendo in my voice and the best sexy expression I could muster. He must have been anticipating my question because he threw a black Adidas sports bag at my feet. Perhaps he thought things were moving too slowly. I opened it and looked in.

"Help yourself," he said nonchalantly. "It might be easier if you empty it."

"Where?"

"On the floor."

I tipped the gear out onto the carpet and started sifting through it. It was mostly leather, rubber, and metal, with an occasional dick pump or handkerchief. There was nothing surprising in the whole mess, but it looked dramatic against the red carpet, like props for a horror film. "Put that cock ring on," he said, "and leave your boots on." He asked me to walk around the room and lean against walls. I kept checking out the room. The curtains were hemmed in a mismatched thread and held together with a pin where they met.

"I like that," he said, referring to my facial expression. I must have been frowning.

I had the idea of getting us into the bedroom to make him cum. I headed toward it and said, "Come in here."

"I like that," he said again. "Tell me what to do." He collected his cigarettes, whiskey, and poppers, squinted his eyes, and said once more, "I like that." He scurried into the bedroom and onto the bed. Ash dropped onto the sheet from the cigarette in his hand. I lay on top of him, focusing on the sheet. Like the couch it was coated with cat hair. I turned my head to the side, facing an ashtray full of cigarette butts. I turned the other way. Now I faced a red plastic foldout chair with a cup of cold tea or coffee on it. Mold floated on top. I closed my eyes and pretended I was somewhere else, in my lovely home, with my lovely baby. This worked long enough to get the job done. He came. I left.

my pride and broken buzzers

Anna Joy Springer

I lost a lot of my old buttery popcorn in my mid-twenties and my buzzers got pretty death defying. My fun house had always been filled with mounds and mounds of buttery popcorn, so now there was all this empty space where the popcorn had been. Everything sagged and swayed. My buzzers looked like used condoms tied off and thrown in the street. Ugly stripey-stripes cut big gashes all over them. They looked like they'd been in an accident with a badly trained tiger. Who'd want to slam their hands down on my deflated buzzers now?

Pushed up in their forced fanfare, they looked fine. I'd roll them up like a hot sticky bun and push them into promotional soda cups. It was when they unfurled that I had problems.

But they weren't as death defying when I was twenty years old and my fun house was full of buttery popcorn. Back then I was shakin' my clam at the amusement park for wall-eyed pickpockets, reading their palms. Everyone always told me that no paying customer likes to enter a fun house stuffed with buttery popcorn, but they were wrong. With my loud, flashy, puffed-up buzzers, I lured all kinds of returning champs into my palm-reading booth at the amusement park for wall-eyed pickpockets. But even stuffed full of buttery popcorn, my buzzers weren't very loud or flashy after I let them loose. Once I got one inside my booth and showed him how to drop his coins into the money catcher, I'd lift one buzzer out and prop it up on the padded forced fanfare. I'd squeeze the "sold" button and pet my pantaloons with one finger, then sneak the buzzer back into its forced fanfare while I distracted the champ by making risk-it-all moves with my tongue near a fake rubber nose on my window. Then, slowly, mesmerized, the champ would offer his sweaty palm, and I'd read it for him. I wouldn't touch the hand; I'd read his fake fortune through bulletproof glass. I'd read it so slowly and so meaningfully, he'd forget all about my hidden buzzers, and drop more coins into the money catcher. We both knew I was lying about his promising future, but that was the scam. I was the unrivalled palm-reading queen of the amusement park for wall-eyed pickpockets, but after two years of conjuring fabulous stories about the lackluster champs' future love, success, and money, I lost my competitive edge. I had no desire to wow. My emu feathers sagged. I poked at myself in the mirror, threw back toxic shots, and grimaced instead of smiling, like there was chicken blood on my teeth. I stood in front of the wavy mirror and could only see the lumpy buttery popcorn filling my fun house. I hated the champs for returning. I hated the whole damn park.

The returning champs watched me get drunker and puffier and meaner at the amusement park for wall-eyed pickpockets, and they stopped coming to get their palms read. Nobody but the foulest suggested an after-hours puppy washing. They couldn't even look at me, let alone beg to slam their hands down on my buzzers for a chance to win it all. I had to leave the razzle-dazzle show. Once I cleared out some of the buttery popcorn from my fun house, I'd go back into business. Maybe I'd start my own puppy-washing gig. I'd be grand. But the truth was I'd always hated crowds and forced cheer. The wall-eyed pickpockets in their embarrassing clown shoes. I'd always hated a parade.

I entered the temporary protection field because I could type. I became an arranger of important white rectangles. I started using an adding machine and a professional tone. I ran in place for half an hour at lunchtime. I covered my fun house with unfreaky costumes from mannequin stores, and I unratted my hair until it looked beaten. I told my buzzers to fuck off between nine and five; they could take a nap or whatever they wanted, but they couldn't flash or make noise.

Once a year, because I became middle class in the temporary protection field, I took my mandatory vacation at a Museum of Survivor Specimens. I became one of those nouveaux, credit-card lesbians who experiments with foreign diversions in survivor museums, because museums turn lesbians into paying spectators, which is highly uncomfortable. We find ourselves craving familiar awe-inspiring tricks. If only those little plastic deer eyes had cameras behind them.

I ended up in the back of a diorama with one of the museum's persistent but creepy diversions. He was a catchy jingle–writer for rip-off tourist attractions. He took me to the hidden part of the dancing bear exhibit, and I hissed but watched myself follow. He kept talking about "the beauty"— the beauty of a dancing bear in a tutu with sleek ankles, the beauty of a good jingle; they were the same thing, he said. I hated the jingle-writer, but there I was behind the taxidermic bear in her dusty crinolines, stuffing his dumb little rubber nose down my throat, gagging, trying to have a cultural experience. Trying to have a familiar awe-inspiring trick. When I took off my forced fanfare, he gasped.

"What happened to you?" He said, pointing at my heart.

"What do you mean?" I asked.

I knew what he meant, but I'd had the same lovely assistant for years and had almost forgotten my buzzers looked broken.

"All those lines, those stripey-stripes?"

"I got attacked by tigers," I said. "At work."

He left in his teeny-tiny car while I was sleeping against a paw-shaped ballet slipper. I had to find my own way out of the carefully organized Museum of Survivor Specimens, without getting caught there and put on display.

When I got back home, I knew it was time to get my buzzers fixed—maybe I could win a brand new washer and dryer set. Then I could start a new puppy-washing business and leave the temporary protection field. A hands-on puppy wash and palm-reading session. I'd encourage my paying spectator to slam his hands down on my buzzers, and we'd stick our fingers in the mouth of the lion. We could risk it all, do everything. No more amusement parks with their safe little bulletproof booths. But first I needed to win the appliances on a game show for the dispossessed, where they'd give me a public repair job.

At the game show for the dispossessed, I met a buzzer repair specialist who was a blood-and-grease wrestler. She gave me a cotton candy blob and made me watch a dynamic training video about the repair job. Full financing was available at 9.8 percent.

I was making $12 an hour in the temporary protection field, but if I could win my brand new washer and dryer set, I'd make some real money, I told her, not just the chump change I got reading palms at the amusement park for wall-eyed pickpockets. I'd pay the loan back presto. I wanted my buzzers sliced, diced, and shiny, ready to work. I wanted to fling off my forced fanfare, to run my fingers over my emu feathers and feel my booby prizes tighten up and shiver like little ballerinas. I'd make the returning champions pay $200 an hour to slam their hands down on my new puffy, fast-singing red alarms and get their puppies washed superclean. The blood-and-grease wrestler said, "That's awe-inspiring."

The video taught me that the blood-and-grease wrestler would carefully cut all the way around my "sold" button and lift it off with special tongs. Then she would stretch the extra stripey tent material out into the air, cut off the extra tent, and sew the "sold" button back on to the newly fitted stripey tent. Presto! Loud flashy buzzers galore! I liked the idea of my "sold" button sitting on a pile of ice in a promotional soda cup, like a fresh pink clam.

They show these repair jobs on afternoon game shows. You can see the dentist tools pulling the stripey-striped tent in weird directions, lifting it off the meat, more like movie-monster mask than living flesh. The buzzer-repair techs give the puppy-washer something hilarious in her IV, and she starts widening then squinching her eyes and smiling like Miss America a little, but stupidly, like she's on a rickety roller-coaster ride toward financial freedom. They cover the puppy-washer's face with a sheet. The stripey tent seems to cut easily, like a canned clam. The sheet over her face is made of pockmarked paper.

The puppy-washer is under there breathing shallowly. If she's awake, like I was at first, she'll try to see the blood-and-grease wrestler's shadow through the dimpled light blue paper but the paper will be opaque. She'll try to make out the sharp tools' strange shapes as the wrestler holds them up to the colored lights. She'll feel the laser cutting around her large affirmation trigger, and she'll smell her stripey tent burning. She'll say, if she can, "I can still feel that."

The blood-and-grease wrestler will say to the blue paper, "You couldn't possibly."

"I do," she'll say, and the paper shroud will jump a little from the force of her breath.

The blood-and-grease wrestler will then lift a giant mallet from her instrument table and ask the puppy-washer, in a parlor tone, "One lump, or two?" The greedy puppy-washer will ask for two lumps of sugar in her make-believe tea. The blood-and-grease wrestler will slam the mallet down twice. The blue paper sheet will quiver, as two elbow-size lumps rise up from the top of the puppy-washer's head, like bald volcanoes.

That's what happened to me, at least. When I got my lumps, I fell backwards down an animal hole and landed in my high school auditorium. A big, hat-wearing cougar was painted in a serenading posture inside an orange circle on the wall behind a basketball hoop. Around the circle, Killer Cougars was painted in jagged, bloody script. The floor of the gym where I landed was wood, high shine. I was unconscious, on a rickety roller-coaster ride to financial independence. Soon the assembly would start.

At the assembly, I was going to win my brand new washer and dryer set so I could make more money as a classy puppy-washer, and all the high school students would watch my buzzer repair. But it wouldn't be a regular game show; it'd be a musical too. It would be an absurdist Brechtian musical about poverty, humiliation, and winning a shiny new job. I'd sing, and the blood-and-grease wrestler would sing too. We'd address the audience directly:

"I want her to cut into me, I want you to watch! This is a musical game show for the dispossessed, of my buzzers getting repaired so I can win a brand new washer and dryer set and go back into showbiz like the cougar, your father!" I spoke-sang emphatically.

271

"She's given me a whole bunch of loot, which she does not possess, in order to fix up her fun house, so she can win a washer and dryer set and get a job that gives her enough loot to pay back her loan. How truly stupid are the masses!" my blood-and-grease wrestler jeered.

I warned the young performers, "Soon you'll have to make everything up from scratch because nobody will tell you the real story anymore! You'll have to build a puzzle of yourself and put it in the mail and hope it gets there."

"Soon you too will be twenty-six years old and all worn out and nobody will want to purchase you for any entertaining purpose, and then you'll come to me, and I will purchase you." My blood-and-grease wrestler started cutting stars and spirals into my thighs with her scalpel, and my hips rose up toward her hand.

I moaned, and turned back toward the crowd, "Soon she will give you a little fright wig cut for your hapless broken buzzers, and you will let yourself be opened up and rearranged which will make your fun house a more desirable shape for returning champions. It will be the first time you'll ever pay to put your fingers in the mouth of the lion with a blood-and-grease wrestler for free!"

"This is a Showcase Showdown for you, young high school performers. To let you know what no one will tell you!" She sang, as she sharpened a toothy saw.

"There's only one reason for this searing pain, like a fist punching meat everywhere inside me, organ-grinding my fun house. There's only one reason I'd ever let myself be sawed in half!"

"There's only one reason she'd let someone hurt her fun house as badly as I'm hurting it now, before your eyes! What is it? What is it? Why are we here now?" The blood-and-grease wrestler (who'd turned into a mustachioed magician in a black silk hat and cape) pulled her giant glinting saw back and forth through my tenderized buzzers.

"Fingers in the mouth of the lion!" the performers in the audience cried out, coming down from the bleachers to quiz show my bonus round and join us in the fabulous conclusion. The gym was so orange, the lights so hot.

"Fingers in the mouth of the lion!!!" the blood-and-grease wrestler and I shouted together, and then we hit crescendo with the performers from the crowd starting to jeer, the high schoolers and I belted out that this must be a musical game show for the dispossessed, not of a rickety rollercoaster ride to financial independence, but a vaudeville act where the archetypal evil magician and his lovely assistant pretend to put their fingers into the mouth of the lion in front of everyone. I was being sawed in half.

Clearly I wanted it, I was the star, and plus, I was paying for it. Since I was paying for it, I must have been enjoying it, so I thrust harder, yelled out louder, so I could hear myself under the blue paper sheet, "Make me disappear you magical blood-and-grease magic-hat fuck! I want my brand new washer and dryer!!!"

As I woke up, I heard the tail end of my show tune. The blue paper was gone. Someone had painted an elaborate sunset on the ceiling of the operating room. There was no serenading cougar, just a dopey sunset. I was wet between my thighs.

"We're almost through," my blood-and-grease wrestler said. I could feel little tugs on my stripey tent as she finished sewing me up.

"Was I screaming obscenely?" I asked.

"You did just fine." The blood-and-grease wrestler announced, not answering.

"No," I pressed her, getting the spins. "I went into this Brechtian musical. I thought I was saying something to you. I'm a little humiliated. I don't know if I really said it out loud," I continued.

"I didn't hear a thing. You might feel some nausea from the anesthesia, just a warning. But you did fine during our rickety roller-coaster ride toward your financial independence."

That was eight years ago. I've since restuffed my fun house full of extra-buttery popcorn, more than ever before. My buzzers are freak shows again, and my booby prizes are literally the size of funnel cakes. The "sold" button itself is flat and wrinkly. The affirmation trigger is light as a scar. The stripey-stripes are less pronounced, but the booby prizes and "sold" button scars are monstrous. I will never again be able show these buzzers to strangers without a warning first, and could never make anyone pay for the privilege. My buzzers are completely death defying, and broken to boot. The right one only perks up when I pinch it really hard, then it stings. The left one responds to a circular rub, but feels creepy, like I'm shorting out, and my "sold" button recoils instead of lighting up. So now my buzzers are these heavy, high-modernist abstractions like the houses of lonely ex–drug wives in the Hollywood hills. When I can, I sit at home holding my tired buzzers, wishing I could still get suicidal. So I lost.

I always knew I was the kind of performer who'd blow my chance at winning a brand new washer and dryer set. I'd wanted that goddamned washer and dryer. I'd wanted to be a puddle of glittery Vaseline and a puppy-washer since I was seven years old. I pulled on my nonexistent booby prizes and told my tissue carnations to grow. I pounded them like Tarzan. I watched performers on the television do exercises to increase the volume of their buzzers, and I did them too. I prayed to Chuck Barris to give me a loud, flashy pair of buzzers so I could be a famous puppy-washer one day. By the time I was in sixth grade, I was wearing a desirable size, like in Pleasures of Evasion magazine.

Chuck Barris answers prayers. Chuck Barris gave me a childhood prize clown who was much older than me with a big hard red nose and a miniature unicycle. Chuck Barris gave me a job at the amusement park for wall-eyed pickpockets so I could pay for my middle-class rehearsals. Chuck Barris gave me my first returning champion who convinced me to go up to his filthy cage after my shift at the drab coffee job.

He told me, "Everyone's a puddle of glittery Vaseline and a puppy-washer, but some are built to win better prizes than others."

I won three pots of Manic Panic that night. He didn't make me disappear, though. We didn't even stick our fingers into the mouth of the lion. He was embarrassed to have such a soft rubber nose. He just waved his wand and said "Ladies and Gentlemen, Welcome to The Greatest Show On Earth!" while I pressed my buzzers into his unguarded vulnerability. His blanket was gray and itchy. He just wanted someone to give him applause. Everyone does.

whoreanomics
Shelby Aesthetic

"**N**o no no!!" It was Ricca yelling at some new girl. "Never ever flip them off when they drive by. They could be honking at your dumb ass 'cause they wanna give you a ride . . . stupid girl! Come over here honey let me give you a lesson in whoreanomics." I started laughing to myself. Ricca took it upon herself to talk to all the newbies who came onto the strip. And she always gave her lesson in whoreanomics in front of as many people as possible. I always thought she did it because it made her feel older or wiser. . . . She says she did 'cause she liked to make sure every girl got turned out right.

She was also quite possibly the most intelligent woman I had ever met.

"What's your name honey?" she asked the new girl.

"Uhh-umm . . . "

"Hold it hold it, right now is lesson number one in whoreanomics. . . . You gotta have a name. And stuttering won't get you anywhere. We all got names over here." She pointed to Rhonda, "You see that shrimp over there with the fake orange tan? That's Oompa. We call her that cause she looks like a goddamn Oompa Loompa." She started howling at her own joke. Ricca was really the one that nicknamed everyone. A new girl would walk up and in a matter of days she had a nickname. She stopped laughing and grabbed TD's arm. "Now this woman. She an old ho. Show some respect to her. We call her TD 'cause she's got the biggest knockers of anyone out here. Triple D." She started laughing again. TD walked off mumbling something. "Come over here Lucy," she waved me over. Shit.

"Yes?" I asked.

"Now this here is Lucy Vulgar. We call her that for two reasons. The first reason is cause she has the filthiest mouth of anyone you will ever meet." I rolled my eyes. Was my mouth really that bad? "The second reason . . . " she was trying to hold back a laugh, "The second reason is cause she always seems to attract the weirdest, nastiest motherfuckers this side of the river." She was rolling on the ground. It was true though, so I didn't say anything.

"Well what about your name?" the new girl asked.

"There isn't anything special about my name. They used to call me Puerto Rico . . . 'cause I'm Puerto Rican, then it shortened to Rico, but I didn't want to sound like a man, so now it's just Ricca." She was pulling herself up off the ground still laughing a little. "Now . . . what's your name?" she asked again.

"It's Jennifer. . . . Nothing special, just Jennifer," she replied.

"Okay, then JJ," Ricca said.

"JJ? I . . . I don't get it, I said my name was Jennifer," she looked at Ricca puzzled.

"You said Just Jennifer. So I am calling you JJ. And now so will everyone else," Ricca said, hands on her hips.

"Okay," JJ said. She looked so scared, and I imagined what I must have looked like the first few nights I came down to the strip. I remembered thinking that all the girls probably never talked to each other, or knew each other. But the truth was they had a strong bond with each other, they really looked out for one another. It made me feel safer.

"Now then, lesson number two in whoreanomics. . . . You see that man walking over there?" JJ looked. "Don't look dummy! Just a glance. You never ever wanna look at any man walking back and forth on that side of street . . . or you will end up on that side of street working for him." Her tone was forceful, you could hear the seriousness of her voice. JJ looked nervous and I knew she understood what Ricca was telling her. "Lesson number three in whoreanomics. . . . You ever get a funny feeling in your stomach about a ride don't go," Ricca's eyes bulged when she said it. "Always trust your instinct honey, if one of these girls tells you not to take a ride with a certain someone . . . listen to them honey, they're not trying to steal your money, they're trying to help you out."

A Johnny pulled up. "Hey girls!" he said, "Who's that?" He was pointing at JJ. We knew this Johnny. He came around two or three times a week.

"I'm . . . uhh . . . JJ" she said.

"You wanna go for a ride JJ?" She was petrified. Her legs were shaking hard. Ricca gave her a nudge, and she moved towards the car. She looked back at her as if to ask, Are you sure? Ricca nudged again. After they drove off Ricca said, "Damn, I guess my lesson in whoreanomics will have to wait till she gets back," she laughed at her own joke. She always laughed at her own jokes. "I need to write a book," she said. "Whoreanomics 101. The Basics of Being a Whore." She laughed hard this time.

I am still waiting for the book.

acknowledgments

Major thanks to Michelle Tea for unending support, advice, and hilarity. To Marie for being the funniest, bitchiest, smartest friend/fishbowl-mate ever. To Sarah Adams, Shane Vogel, Molly, and Kevin Walter for feedback. Inspiration and assistance: Carol Leigh, Amber Dawn, Chris Kraus, Greg Taylor, Jeri Beard, Tre Vasquez, and Bruce Springsteen. Thanks to Tennessee Jones for instigating this project. And thanks to my fabulous editor at Seal, Brooke Warner.

about the contributors

SHELBY AESTHETIC is an artist/writer/film documenter. Shelby has done sex work at various times in her life as a means of survival, and is currently a sex worker activist. She moved to Alabama in 1998 and is currently doing outreach for sex workers, documenting their lives, and writing for her own underground zine *Psycho Tomato*. Her book *Dick's Favorite Goods* will be published through Little Lies, Unrepentant Publishers next year. Shelby is a supporter/believer in equality for all people. "As long as those in the sex industry are pushed further into the shadows, more rapes, violent acts and murders will take place. . . . How long are we going to sit around while men and women are losing their lives? Decriminalize prostitution!!!"

JENNIFER BLOWDRYER got her name from The Blowdry-
ers, a punk band she sang with in 1979 in San Francisco. The
name has continued on as, stunningly enough, has she. She
received her MFA from Columbia's writing division in 1988
and pioneered Smut Fests the same year at Harmony Bur-
lesque in New York City, and her most recent books include
Good Advice for Young Trendy People Of All Ages (San Francisco,
CA: Manic D Press, 2005), and *The Revolution of 1964* (Berkeley, CA: Zeitgeist Press, 2007), a book of poems by her and
her mom Lenore. She is bicoastal, bimonthly, and not hard to
find. Listen to her tunes on Myspace, or see www.jennifer-
blowdryer.com for outdated tour information.

SIOBHAN BROOKS is a PhD candidate at New School University in sociology. Her writings have appeared in several
anthologies and journals, in *Feminism and Anti-Racism: International Struggles for Justice* and *Anti-Racism: International
Struggles for Justice* (France Winddance Twine and Kathleen
Blee, eds., New York: NYU Press, 2001) and University of
California, *Hastings's Women's Law Journal*, Winter 1999. She
is currently finishing her dissertation, which looks at sexual-
ized desire, or erotic capital, as a variable in racial segregation
among black/latina women in housing, education, and sex
industry jobs by analyzing social stratification within strip
clubs in New York and San Francisco. She is a lecturer in

Univerity of California, Santa Barbara's Women Studies and Law and Society programs.

VAGINAL DAVIS is an originator of the homo-core punk movement and a genderqueer art-music icon. Her concept bands—including Pedro Muriel and Esther, Cholita! The Female Menudo, black fag, and the Afro Sisters—have left an indelible mark on the development of underground music. Set apart from gallery-centered art and Hollywood movies, and from those systems' necessities of high-polish, low-substance production, Vaginal Davis's low-budget—often no-budget—performance, experimental film, and video practice has critiqued exclusionary conceits from the outside. Vaginal Davis is the key proponent of the disruptive performance aesthetic known as terrorist drag. Disrupting the cultural assimilation of gay-oriented and corporate-friendly drag, she positions herself at an uncomfortable tangent to the conservative politics of gay culture, mining its contradictory impulses to interrupt the entrenchment of its assimilatory strategies. A self-labeled "sexual repulsive," Ms. Davis consistently refuses to ease conservative tactics within gay and black politics, employing punk music, invented biography, insults, self-mockery, and repeated incitements to group sexual revolt—all to hilarious and devastating effect. Her body a car-crash of excessive significations, Vaginal Davis stages a clash of identifications within and against both heterosexual and queer cultures, and black and hispanic identities.

AMBER DAWN (a.k.a. Trala La) is a grassroots darling, writer, and performance artist based in Vancouver, Canada. Her first book, an anthology of femme-written porn titled *With A Rough Tongue* (Vancouver, BC: Arsenal Pulp Press, 2005), was nominated for an Independent Publishers Award. Her genderfuck docuporn, *Girl on Girl*, screened in eight countries, has been added to the gender studies curriculum at Concordia University, Montreal. She organizes an annual FTM top-surgery fundraiser, "For The Boys." She is the editor of and writing mentor for a zine written by and for male and transgendered street workers. After more than fifteen years of survival-turned-sex work, she is now employed as a sexual health educator at Western Canada's oldest AIDS service organization and is working on her second book—a magical realism novel.

STEPHEN ELLIOTT is a former stripper and the author of six books, including *Happy Baby* (San Francisco, CA: McSweeney's Books, 2004), a finalist for the New York Public Library's Young Lion Award, as well as a best book of 2004 in salon.com, *Newsday*, *Chicago New City*, the *Journal News*, and *The Village Voice*. His most recent book is an almost all true sexual memoir called *My Girlfriend Comes to the City and Beats Me Up* (San Francisco, CA: Cleis Press, 2006). His work has been featured in *Esquire, The New York Times, GQ, Best American Non-Required Reading, Best American Erotica*, and *Best Sex Writing 2006*. He is the founder of the Progressive Reading Series and the executive director of LitPAC, a literary political action committee.

JANELLE GALAZIA is a stripper and hooker and daydreamer. She loves to write and think and make money. She has no special credits to her name, but is constantly trying to live up to the image she had of her adult self when she was a child.

Born and raised in Chicago, former hair-metal fanatic ANA J started verbalizing her inner demons in 1995. After a few years of self-publishing her stories in zines and corunning an independent zine distro, she moved to Olympia, Washington where she continued to self-publish. She collaborated through the years with many other artists and performers she didn't really keep track of. Upon returning to Chicago, she joined forces with Ms. Nomy Lamm to create and cohost The Finger, a highly successful, all-inclusive monthly queer variety show. She has in the past performed with Sister Spit, cohosted countless drag shows, and toured with the Sex Workers Art Show in

2004. Ana J has been involved in the seedy underbelly of the adult carnival for the past nine years, the past six as a professional dominatrix. She currently resides in Tucson, Arizona where she is employed as a baker and is working on a comic/cookbook/book. She spends most of her time collecting owl-related bric-a-brac and browsing the aisles of grocery stores aimlessly for hours without making a single purchase.

JUBA KALAMKA is a producer, curator, essayist, and consensus H.N.I.C. of the western hemisphere. He is the creator of the microlabel and distro Sugartruck Recordings, is a founding member of the award-winning homohop crew Deep Dickollective (D/DC). Kalamka is the director of the PeaceOUT World Homohop Festival in Oakland, California, which celebrates its seventh year in 2007 and has spawned sister events in New York City, Atlanta, and London, England. Kalamka is featured in the homohop documentary Pick Up The Mic and recently completed an MFA in Poetics at New College of California in San Francisco. He lives in Oakland with his primary partner, their daughter, and a love-mongering cat. He practices polyamory both locally and globally.

EMI KOYAMA puts the emi back in feminism at http://eminism.org.

CHRIS KRAUS is the author of the novels *Torpor* (Cambridge, MA: MIT Press, 2006), *Aliens & Anorexia* (Cambridge, MA: MIT Press, 2000), and a collection of essays about the Los Angeles art world, *Video Green: Los Angeles Art and the Triumph of Nothingness* (New York, NY: Semiotext(e), 2004). She is the coeditor of *Hatred of Capitalism.* She has written on art, poetics, and theory for academic anthologies and art magazines. Kraus is the founding editor of Semiotext(e)'s Native Agents imprint.

BRUCE LABRUCE is a writer, filmmaker, and photographer stuck in the gulag otherwise known as Toronto, Canada. He started out as a child, then quickly moved on to the production of homo punk fanzines (*J.D.s* [with G.B. Jones], *Dumb Bitch Deserves To Die* [with Candy Parker]) and Super-8 mm movies. These products helped to launch the so-called homo-core or queer-core movement, which corrupted a whole new generation of homosexuals. LaBruce's early films, *No Skin Off My Ass* and *Super 8 1/2* went on to become cult hits and film festival circuit favorites, earning slots in such high-profile fests as Sundance, London, Berlin, Dublin, Thessaloniki, Toronto, Vancouver, San Francisco, and Tokyo. LaBruce's *Hustler White*, made in collaboration with Rick Castro, premiered at Sundance and similarly went on to become a film festival and cult favorite, winning the grand prize at the International Trash Film Festival. Hustler was followed by his first legitimate porn film, *Skin Flick*. LaBruce's photography and writing has appeared in a wide range of publications including *Honcho, Inches, Index Magazine, Eye Magazine, The National Post, The UK Guardian, Dutch, Butt, Strut, Dazed and Confused, Loyal, The Breeder, Bon,* and *K48*. He has also produced two books, *The Reluctant Pornographer* (1997), his premature memoirs, from Gutter Press, and *Ride, Queer, Ride* (1997), a survey of his work from Plug-In Books.

NOMY LAMM is a writer, singer, and self-taught accordion player. She began writing zines at age seventeen, focusing on body-hatred and the systems that enforce it. In the fourteen years since then she has written, performed, and organized around queerness, body image, trauma and disability, feminism, trans inclusion, radical Jewish identity, antiracist ally work, and more. Her writing has been published in numerous feminist anthologies including *Listen Up: Voices from the Next Feminist Generation* (Barbara Findlen, ed., Seattle, WA: Seal Press, 2001) and *Body Outlaws: Writings on Body Image and Identity* (Ophira Edut, ed., Seattle, WA: Seal Press, 2000). She writes an advice column for the feminist magazine *make/shift*, and is currently working on her first novel.

ARIEL SMITH is an award-winning filmmaker and video artist who has been creating her own independent works since 2001, many of which have screened at festivals internationally. Her most recent works include *1, 2, 3 KnockUP* (2006, DV) and *Savior Complex* (2007, 16mm) She currently resides in Ottawa by way of Vancouver and Montreal.

GLORIA LOCKETT is the former codirector of the prostitutes rights organization COYOTE (Call Off Your Old Tired Ethics) and Executive Director of the California Prostitute Education Project (CAL-PEP), an Oakland-based, nonprofit AIDS and HIV prevention organization that works with street prostitutes. Lockett served on San Francisco District Attorney Terence Hallinan's Task Force on Prostitution and as a member of former Governor George Deukmejian's California AIDS Leadership Task Force. She has been published in several anthologies, including *The Black Women's Health Book: Speaking for Ourselves*, edited by Evelyn C. White (Seattle, WA: Seal Press, 1990), *Sex Work: Writings by Women in the Sex Industry*, edited by Frederique Delacoste and Priscilla Alexander (San Francisco, CA: Cleis Press, 1984), and *Lessons from the Damned: Queers, Whores and Junkies Respond to AIDS*, by Nancy Stoller (New York: Routledge, 1998). She was also, for eighteen years, a prostitute.

NAIMA LOWE creates films, performances, and writings that consistently defy genre and explore the complex relationships between racial identity, collective memory, the body, and queer sexuality. Naima's work has been featured in the Sex Workers Art Show, The Philadelphia Fringe Festival, and at Rites and Reason Theatre in Providence, Rhode Island. Her recent film, *Birthmarks*, a thirty-minute experimental documentary about her father witnessing the 1967 Newark Riots, has been selected to travel the country and the world as part of NextFrame, an international touring festival of student films. Naima graduated from Brown University with a BA in Africana Studies in 2002, and is completing her MFA in Film and Media Arts from Temple University. Naima has two cats and misses the ocean.

JESSICA MELUSINE is a writer, model, and bon vivant featured in *Paying for It, Shameless, Zaftig Glamour Girls: Femme/Femme Erotica*, and a performer at Perverts Put Out! and assorted Ladyfests. Her story *Avatar in Pink* appears in *Red Light: Superheroes, Saints, and Sluts* (Vancouver: Arsenal Pulp Press, 2004); the book has been nominated for both a Lambda Award and an IPPY.

VERONICA MONET offers workshops, lectures, and professional advice on sex and relationships. Veronica Monet's *Sex Secrets of Escorts: Tips from a Pro* (New York, NY: Alpha Books, 2005) is available in most major bookstores. Her extensive media credits include CNN, A&E, ABC's 20/20, FOX News, Bill Maher's Politically Incorrect and *The New York Times*. Monet was educated at Oregon State University, graduating with honors as a psychology major. Monet is also published in six books including a textbook, *Human Sexuality: Opposing Viewpoints* (St. Paul, MN: Greenhaven Press, 1995), *Whores and Other Feminists* (New York, NY: Routledge, 1997), *Breaking Ritual Silence* (Gardnerville, TN: Trout and Sons, 1998), *Porn 101* (Amherst, NY: Prometheus Books, 1999), *Dangerous Families: Queer Writing on Surviving* (New York, NY: Harrington Park Press, 2004) and *Paying for It* (Oakland, CA: Greenery Press, 2004). Monet has over a decade of experience with the practical and political aspects of sex work, having worked as an erotic model, porn actress, prostitute, escort, and courtesan. Her political activism includes volunteer work for Bay Area Bisexual Network, COYOTE San Francisco, and Sex Worker Outreach Project. Ms. Monet is a Certified Sex Educator (SFSI), a founding member of the Association of Sexual Energy Professionals (ASEP), a trained volunteer for the Center Against Rape and Domestic Violence (CARDV) and an Ordained Minister (ULC). Her next book promises a departure from the sex-manual genre while maintaining her uncompromising passion for exploring sensible alternatives to society's sacred cows. Please visit www.flossophy. net for clues.

EILEEN MYLES has written thousands of poems since she gave her first reading at CBGB's in 1974. *BUST* magazine calls her "the rock star of modern poetry" and *The New York Times* says she's "a cult figure to a generation of post-punk females forming their own literary avant-garde." Eileen headed to New York after college (University of Massachusetts, Boston), quickly gaining the friendship of Allen Ginsberg, working for poet James Schuyler, becoming a habitué of the household of Ted Berrigan and Alice Notley, and generally being a notable part of the turbulent punk and art scene that animated Manhattan's East Village. From 1977–1979, she edited the poetry magazine, *dodgems*. From 1984–1986, she was artistic director of St. Mark's Poetry Project. She also wrote, acted in, and directed plays at St. Mark's and PS 122. Always, she has been a virtuoso performer of her own work—she's read to audiences at colleges, performance spaces, and bookstores across America as well as in Europe, Iceland, and Russia. In 1992, she conducted an openly female write-in campaign for president of the United States. In 1997, Eileen toured with Sister Spit Ramblin' Road Show. Her books include *Sorry, Tree* (Seattle, WA: Wave Books, 2007), *Skies* (Santa Rosa, CA: Black Sparrow Press, 2001), *on my way* (Newton, MA: Faux Press, 2001), *Cool for You* (New York, NY: Soft Skull Press, 2000), *School of Fish* (Santa Rosa, CA: Black Sparrow Press, 1997), *Maxfield Parrish* (Santa Rosa, CA: Black Sparrow Press, 1995),

293

Not Me (New York, NY: Semiotext(e), 1991), and *Chelsea Girls* (Santa Rosa, CA: Black Sparrow Press, 1994). In 1995, with Liz Kotz, she edited *The New Fuck You/Adventures in Lesbian Reading* (New York, NY: Semiotext(e), 1995). She's a frequent contributor to *Book Forum*, *Art in America*, *The Village Voice*, *The Nation*, *The Stranger*, *Index*, and *Nest*.

BLAKE NEMEC is a media activist, phlebotomist, and sound engineer. His writing has been published in *San Francisco Bay Times*, *slingshot*, *Lip Magazine*, as well as in two anthologies, *From the Inside Out* (San Francisco, CA: Manic D Press, 2004) and *That's Revolting!* (Brooklyn, NY: Soft Skull Press, 2004). He is a sound technician with five years' dedication to national microradio and independent media groups. He has worked as a boom operator and sound engineer in various independent films including *Dear Doctors: Born Queer.*

KIRK READ is the author of *How I Learned to Snap* (Athens, GA: Hill Street Press, 2001), a memoir about being openly gay in a small Virginia high school. *Snap* was named an Honor Book by the American Library Association. Read spent two years touring to 120 cities and towns to spread the gospel of sexed-up heavy metal queer teenagers. He is working on a novel and a memoir about sex work called *This is the Thing.* He frequently performs at colleges around the country and hosts spoken-word events around San Francisco, including the open mics Smack Dab and K'vetch. He is a longtime counselor and phlebotomist at St. James Infirmary, San Francisco's free health clinic for current and former sex workers. At the infirmary, he started a support group for male sex workers in 1999 and was volunteer coordinator. This semester, he finishes his MFA in Creative Writing at San Francisco State University and is the apprentice of a gourmet organic chef. He's a southern gentleman and a witch.

Although AIDEN SHAW first became familiar to many people as a porn star, he has also directed music videos, designed websites, and worked as a photographer, model, actor, singer/ songwriter, and interior designer. Shaw is the author of three novels, *Brutal* (1996), *Boundaries* (1999), and *Wasted* (2001), all of which received widespread attention in British and U.S. gay media. In 1991 he collaborated with fine artist Mark Beard to produce a handmade, limited edition book that is now housed in the Metropolitan Museum of Modern Art. Shaw is also the author of a 1997 volume of poetry, *If Language at the Same Time Shapes and Distorts our Ideas and Emotions, How do we Communicate Love?* His autobiography, *My Undoing*, was released to wide acclaim in 2007. Read more about him on his website, www.aidenshaw.com.

SISTER GRIMM is a writer, performer, polyglot, traveler and teacher. She is currently teaching in the land of modern windmills and northern lights, and working on a full-length poetry manuscript.

MIRHA-SOLEIL ROSS is a transsexual performer, video maker, sex worker, and activist who grew up amongst mountains of scrap, sewer rats, and bottles of gin in Notre-Dame du Sacre Coeur, a poor district situated on the South Shore of Montreal, Quebec. She has been working and living in Toronto since 1992. Since 1993, she has created over a dozen videos (including *Tremblement de Chair*, *G-SPrOuT!*, *Allo Performance*), which have been screened at film festivals across Canada, the U.S., and Europe. She is the founder of MEAL-TRANS, the first ever publicly funded multiservices, peer-run program for low-income and street-active transsexual and transgendered people in Toronto. Ross's show *Yapping Out Loud: Contagious Thoughts from an Unrepentant Whore* premiered as part of the MAYWORKS Festival of Working People and the Arts. She is interviewed under the name of Jeanne B. in Shannon Bell's book *Whore Carnival* (New York, NY: Autonomedia, 1995), and as Mirha-Soleil Ross in Viviane Namaste's *Sex Change, Social Change: Reflections on Identities, Institutions, and Nations* (Toronto: Women's Press, 2005). She appears in *Bent on Writing: Contemporary Queer Tales* (Toronto:

Women's Press, 2002), and in *My Breasts, My Choice: Journeys Through Surgery* (Toronto: Sumach Press, 2003).

ANNA JOY SPRINGER has little fangs and barks like a deer when excited. Teenage fans call her "The Bird Lady," because she writes, almost exclusively, about birds. Before moving to San Diego to teach at Eileen Myles's School for Wayward Writers, she did lots of femme jobs, made neon sculptures, sang in legendary punk bands Blatz, The Gr'ups, and Cypher in the Snow, and read her purple prose with Sister Spit. She currently tongue-lashes misogynists, writes weird and lengthy cross-genre messes, and ponders the many species of love, radical performative pedagogy, and the gyre of ethics in konsumer kapitalism.

MATTILDA, A.K.A. MATT BERNSTEIN SYCAMORE, is the editor of *Nobody Passes: Rejecting the Rules of Gender and Conformity* (Emeryville, CA: Seal Press, 2006) and an expanded second edition of *That's Revolting! Queer Strategies for Resisting Assimilation* (Brooklyn, NY: Soft Skull Press, 2004). *The Night That Plays like Ping-Pong in My Head* is excerpted from Mattilda's first novel, *Pulling Taffy* (San Francisco, CA: Suspect Thoughts Press, 2003). Her second novel, *So Many Ways to Sleep Badly*, will be published by City Lights in fall/winter 2008, and Mattilda hopes that it will destroy literature.

Her first anthology, *Tricks and Treats: Sex Workers Write About Their Clients* (New York, NY: Harrington Park Press, 2000), was recently translated into Italian. Mattilda loves feedback. Her blog is nobodypasses.blogspot.com and her homepage is www.mattbernsteinsycamore.com.

Writer, performer, and literary-event wrangler MICHELLE TEA is cofounder of the original Sister Spit experience, the legendary all-girl spoken-word road show. She is the author of four memoirs, including *The Chelsea Whistle* (New York, NY: Seal Press, 2002), the award-winning *Valencia* (Seattle, WA: Seal Press, 2000), and the illustrated *Rent Girl* (San Francisco, CA: Last Gasp, 2004), as well as her first novel, *Rose of No Man's Land* (San Francisco, CA: MacAdam/Cage Press, 2006). She is currently at work on the graphic novel *Carrier*, illustrated by Laurenn McCubbin and set to be published in 2007 by MacAdam/Cage Press. Michelle has edited three anthologies, most recently *Baby, Remember My Name: New Queer Girl Writings* (New York, NY: Carroll and Graf, 2006).

TRE VASQUEZ, two spirit, former ho, down for reclaiming our histories and spiritual wellness through hip-hop. He uses performance and other mediums of art as an offering to an indigenous movement of young warriors/soldiers in order to take back our land, communities, hearts, minds, and bodies. He has performed in many events such as The Sex Worker Art Festival Tucson, Intercourse: A Sex and Gender Recipe for Revolution, a tour with the band Tricrotic, and a whole lot of shows that are none of your business. Keeping it spiritual, keeping it political, keeping it gangsta by any and all means necessary.

SHOSHANA VON BLANCKENSEE is a native San Franciscan, a veteran of the Sister Spit Ramblin' Road Show, who has been featured at The Coco Club, The Chameleon (remember those ole places), The Paradise Lounge, and K'vetch (at Sadie's Flying Elephant). She also coran a reading series at The Bearded Lady Cafe (yet another place that doesn't exist anymore). She is the author of a play, *Show Me Your Arms*, which went up in March 2000 in a little theater called Bindlestiff, and the star of the lesbo mommy movie *Playdate*, which came out in last year's Frameline festival. She has been published in *On Our Backs* (Los Angeles, CA: Alyson Books, 2004) and the anthology *Bottoms Up!* (Brooklyn, NY: Soft Skull Press, 2004).

ANA VOOG is an omnisexual Minneapolis-based multimedia performance artist. At this time she is most known for her 24/7 in-home webcam, which is now the longest-running homecam on the net. Thee modern grrl is infotainment value:

Ana Voog becomes sexual stereotypes and then blows them up from the inside out—knowledge through nonsense. By doing and being what sexual stereotypes are not supposed to she hopes these roles will be abandoned and new ideas will spring forth. Now, as she nears age 40, she has been through many incarnations as an artist. First as painter and musician on her eleven-year journey as singer/songwriter of the all-female band The Blue Up, which brought forth five records on two major labels. Second as "camgirl," photographer/pornographer and writer/documentarian, which brought her worldwide recognition from the Museum of Modern Art in New York City, *The New York Times*, *A&E*, *Playboy*, *Hard Copy*, etc. Thirdly, she's become almost a recluse in North America, crocheting avant-garde hats and spinning yarn from exotic animals and futuristic textiles. Say wha? Fourthly, after all this she says, Jedi-style, "I emerge still a cocoon" now at the end of her beginning, she starts . . . just like the paradox she is. She can be found at www.anacam.com.

about the editor

© KARL GIANT

Annie Oakley is an activist, artist, and curator, as well as a ten-year sex industry veteran. Oakley created and continues to organize the Sex Workers Art Show Tour, a nationally acclaimed cabaret-style show featuring visual and performance art by sex workers. She has lectured and performed at colleges and theatres across the country, and is a firm believer in cultural production as activism. For more information, please visit www.sexworkersartshow.com.

Selected Titles from Seal Press

For more than thirty years, Seal Press has published groundbreaking books. By women. For women. Visit our website at www.sealpress.com

INDECENT: HOW I MAKE IT AND FAKE IT AS A GIRL FOR HIRE by Sarah Katherine Lewis. $14.95, 1-58005-169-3. An insider reveals the gritty reality behind the alluring façade of the sex industry.

NOBODY PASSES: REJECTING THE RULES OF GENDER AND CONFORMITY edited by Mattilda, a.k.a Matt Bernstein Sycamore. $15.95, 1-58005-184-7. A timely and thought-provoking collection of essays that confronts and challenges the notion of belonging by examining the perilous intersections of identity, categorization, and community.

BARE: THE NAKED TRUTH ABOUT STRIPPING by Elisabeth Eaves. $14.95, 1-58005-121-9. A closer look at the way sexuality is viewed in our culture: what, if anything, constitutes "normal" desire; the ethics of swapping money—or anything else—for sex.

GETTING OFF: A WOMAN'S GUIDE TO MASTURBATION by Jamye Waxman, illustrations by Molly Crabapple. $14.94, 1-58005-219-3. Empowering and female-positive, this is a comprehensive guide for women on the history and mechanics of the oldest and most common sexual practice.

CUNT: A DECLARATION OF INDEPENDENCE by Inga Muscio. $14.95, 1-58005-075-1. "An insightful, sisterly, and entertaining exploration of the word and the part of the body it so bluntly defines. Ms. Muscio muses, reminisces, pokes into history and emerges with suggestions for the understanding of—and reconciliation with—what it means to have a cunt."—Roberta Gregory, author of *Naughty Bitch*

NAKED ON THE INTERNET by Audacia Ray. $15.95, 1-58005-209-2. Sex rights advocate reveals that many young women use the Internet to explore their desire and develop their sexual identities.